RENAISSANCE WOMEN

Nuns, Sultanas and Queens Legitimising Female Sovereignty

METIN MUSTAFA

Essays Series

Centre for Ottoman Renaissance and Civilisation
Sydney
©2021

Copyright ©2021 by Centre for Ottoman Renaissance and Civilisation

All rights reserved. No part of this book may be reproduced or transmitted in any form or by any means, electronic or mechanical, including photocopying, recording or by any information storage and retrieval system without permission in writing from the Publisher and Author.

Published by Centre for Ottoman Renaissance and Civilisation

Email: info@ottomanrenaissance.org

Website: ottomanrenaissance.org

ISBN: 978-0-646-83543-3

Printed in the United States

Cover design by Centre for Ottoman Renaissance and Civilisation. Portrait of Hürrem (Roxelana) Sultan by 18th century anonymous painter.

To my mother ~

her presence still continues to inspire me

Other books by the author:

Michelangelo meets Sinan:
Representations of the Divine, Salvation and Paradise in Renaissance Art

History of Ottoman Renaissance Art:
From Mehmed I to Selim II. Revised Edition.

The Ottoman Renaissance:
A Reconsideration of Early Modern Ottoman Art, 1413-1575

Tragedy of Sultan Süleyman (a play)

Contents

Preface	xi
1. Renaissance Women's Patronage ~ A Comparative Reading of Early Modern Women's Patronage in Italy and Ottoman Istanbul *ESSAY I*	1
Bibliography	43
2. Negotiating Gender in the Early Modern Period ~ The illusion of seclusion and the metaphors of Ottoman imperial women's sovereignty *ESSAY II*	47
Bibliography	73
3. Two Queens, Three Letters and Three Gifts ~ Metaphors of the visual language of female sovereignty in the Early Modern Period *ESSAY III*	77
Bibliography	93
4. 'Siyer-i Nebi' and the Early Modern Ottoman representations of Muslim Women *ESSAY IV*	97
Bibliography	117
Notes	121

Preface

This book is the first part of the essays series that grew out of my doctorate years between 2103 and 2017. My research interests in the idea of many renaissances and cross-cultural interactions in the early modern Mediterranean world between the Ottomans and Europeans provided me with ample scope to delve into multiple aspects of Renaissance cultures of the sixteenth century. The content is of historical significance because it draws on comparative analysis of the accomplishments of early modern women in Europe and the Ottoman world respectively.

To insist on an exclusively Florentine, Italian, or European *rinascita* or cultural rebirth would fail to appreciate the cultural interconnectedness of the early modern period. In contrast, by recognising Ottoman arts as part of a larger Renaissance narrative the three essays celebrate the achievements of the women of the Renaissance and presents a more objective version of the historical and cultural contexts of the sixteenth-century Mediterranean. This short exploration of early modern women and their contributions to the Mediterranean *zeitgeist* makes a contribution to existing scholarship by recognising the significance of sixteenth century Ottoman imperial women with their European counterparts. By reorienting the purview, a greater under-

PREFACE

standing of Renaissance women can be achieved, ultimately broadening our understanding of early modern history.

The three essays in this book place more emphasis on the role of early modern women in the Ottoman imperial *harem* and their counterparts in Italy, influential wives and nuns. The discussion also engages in the correspondence between Safiye Sultan and Elizabeth I establishing connections between the Ottoman and English royal households further reinforcing the legitimising of female sovereignty during the Renaissance. The predominant focus on the patronage of Renaissance women in asserting their sovereignty and challenging the patriarchal norms of early modern societies underpin the significance of the role of influential women in Ottoman Istanbul, Italy and England. I argue this through the feminist paradigm and the idea of mimicry put forward by the French philosopher Luce Irigaray. The importance of this demonstrates women were not silent, but active participants in early modern societies in Europe and the Ottoman Empire.

Dr. Metin Mustafa

Centre for Ottoman Renaissance and Civilisation

24 February 2021

Renaissance Women's Patronage ~ A Comparative Reading of Early Modern Women's Patronage in Italy and Ottoman Istanbul

ESSAY 1

Abstract: This essay aims to articulate on the analogies of the patronage of influential wives and nuns of Renaissance Italy and those of Ottoman Imperial women of Renaissance Istanbul. From this study, there emerge similar practices in early modern women of the sixteenth century asserting their power and authority through architectural symbolisms. From a gendered architectural perspective, the assertiveness of female agency subverts the norms of patriarchy of the early modern period. Furthermore, through the feminist lens, the article demonstrates the *presence of absence* of these influential women making them proactive participants in early modern social dynamics.

Keywords: *Ottoman Empire, Renaissance, women, patronage, architecture, sovereignty*

The sixteenth century Ottoman imperial architect Sinan built numerous mosques for Ottoman royal women. This article explores how Sinan accommodated his art to represent his female patrons. Although Sultan Süleyman's wife Hürrem Sultan set a precedent for sixteenth century Ottoman women builders, it was her daughter Mihrimah Sultan and daughter-in-law Nurbanu Sultan, who elevated the status of imperial women and their presence in the Ottoman Empire with their imperial mosque complexes in Istanbul. This article serves two purposes: firstly, it focuses on the gendered architectural patronage of Ottoman royal women; secondly, it draws on the comparisons with their Renaissance counterparts in Italy to demonstrate similar practices of early modern women's patronage. By comparing the gendered architectural patronage of Ottoman royal women in Renaissance Istanbul to the women of Renaissance Italy a similar pattern begins to emerge where female agency no longer remains reticent in a patriarchal norm. Here emerges the assertion of female 'self' through architectural representations. In this way, the interaction of male / female networks in the higher echelons of early modern societies at least, tend to lose meaning altogether.

Methodology

Both Leslie Pierce and Lucienne Thys-Senocak make a distinction between the 'invisibility' of the charitable acts of women, i.e., through their endowments of mosques, and the 'visibility' of the physical structures of the buildings they commissioned. This argument, however, suggests that the former acts had less permanent impact than the buildings, namely because of the large spaces they occupy, which conveyed the women's representational presence to the masses.[1] Accordingly, D. Fairchild Ruggles has suggested that, "the buildings stand, in the sense of synecdoche, in place of their donors, and enjoy a public profile denied to the woman herself. Perhaps it is also because charitable acts, although witnessed by society, are recorded in those centuries in texts written by men, so that women may appear to have no agency and are therefore 'absent'."[2]

Luce Irigaray, a French feminist-philosopher, states that in order for women from history to assign to the feminine they had to resort to "mimicry", and convert "a form of subordination into an affirmation, and thus to begin to thwart it".[3] According to Irigaray, women demand to speak as a masculine "subject", and through mimesis, a woman attempts to recover her place from exploitation by discourse: "without allowing herself to be simply reduced to it. It means to resubmit herself – inasmuch as she is on the side of the "perceptible" of "matter" – to "ideas" in particular to ideas about herself, that are elaborated in/by a masculine logic."[4] By applying this *universal* interpretation to Ottoman imperial woman of the sixteenth and seventeenth centuries, it may be argued that through their architectural patronage, the imperial women demonstrated the subversion of the Ottoman patriarchal social order, and negated being "products" for use and exchange by men.[5] This exercise of power in the hands of women signified the changing political attitudes in a predominantly male dominated hierarchy.

Reversal of gender power in a patriarchal is evident through architectural representations by women. In the introduction to *Architecture and Feminism*, Deborah Coleman asks, "[w]hat role does architectural discourse itself play in preserving gender-based relations of power?"[6] The difficulty, she stresses, in attempting to answer this is to risk revealing the complicity of architectural discourse in the struggles over the mobility and social space granted to women.[7] Indeed, the limited social space granted to Ottoman imperial women is crucial to fully understanding their patronage and assertion of power. Similarly, interpreting Plato and Jacques Derrida, in her essay titled "Women, Chora, Dwelling", Elizabeth Grosz states that Plato's featureless, neutral, but altogether necessary "bridge" between the world of Forms or Ideas and material reality can be understood as the basis for the engendering of the intelligible world. She highlights the "unacknowledged and unrepayable debt that the very notion of space, and the built environment that relies on its formulation, owe to what Plato characterizes as the 'femininity' of the chora".[8] Grosz also aligns her argument with Irigaray's reading of the history of philosophy as the erasure of women's autonomy and worth:

Irigaray claims that masculine modes of thought have performed a devastating sleight of hand: they have obliterated the debt they owe to the most primordial of all spaces, the maternal space from which all subjects emerge, and which they ceaselessly attempt to usurp [...] The production of a [male] world – the construction of an 'artificial' or cultural environment, the production of an intelligible universe, religion, philosophy, the creation of true knowledge and valid practices of and in that universe – is implicated in the systematic and violent erasure of the contributions of women, femininity and the maternal. This erasure is the foundation or ground on which thoroughly masculine world is built.[9]

However, the absence of Ottoman imperial women in visual material was not exactly a simple act of subordination. If, as Coleman suggests, it was "the total eclipsing of the feminine."[10] Despite doing so from a restricted space, the financial power at their disposal gave them the freedom to undertake expensive building projects, and therefore, demonstrate their presence in society. It may seem that they were merely objects of male sexual gratification; this was clearly not the case.

Contextual understanding of the patronage of Renaissance Women

Women of Renaissance Italy, like their Ottoman counterparts in Renaissance Istanbul, were also influential in asserting their presence. However, just as traditionalist scholarship views the women of the *harem* as being oppressed and suppressed, the same view is also held about the women of the Renaissance where, as Chojnacki states, "the structures of patriarchy, the organized and enduring campaign of men and institutions [...] restrict[ed] women's experience by implementing the ideology of male dominance."[11] To an extent, this may have been true in both Venice and the Ottoman Empire, and is supported by an example offered by Chojnacki, "the women of Morosini as being so important to their families, and having such substantial legal and economic resources, that they could influence the behaviour of their male kin, natal and marital, and on that basis contribute to the cohesion of the patriciate – the achievements of these women cannot be assessed through the ways in which they managed to exercise agency under the patriarchal umbrella".[12] Similarly, Bursa records from the early seventeenth century contain details of a warehouse that belonged to an Ottoman merchant woman, who traded on a substantial scale and whose business she may have inherited from her merchant father.[13] What the accomplishments of such women indicate is that they made choices and employed wealth, and influenced both men and women. Hürrem Sultan was exemplary in these areas, and according to Chojnacki, Süleyman and Hürrem had carved out "individual spheres of autonomous action."[14] However, in terms of wealth under Islamic law, Ottoman women had full rights to their inheritance and dowry, which could use in almost any way she chose. This was markedly different from other early modern societies in which male power 'guarded' women's property. In relation to women's wealth, King suggests the following: "This power was carefully guarded in the Renaissance centuries, and indeed extending itself, to the detriment of women's status.

The paradox that women could possess property yet not control it is central to an understanding of women's place. That place was at the intersection of two lineages (the family as defined by descent through male heads from a male ancestor), belonging to none."[15] While Renaissance women had the right to acquire wealth through their dowries and inheritance, in the case of Morosini women the women could not dispose of their wealth. Instead it remained within the family, as evidenced by the legacy of Giovanni di Morosini (in his 1397 will), who left "10,000 ducats' worth of shares in the monte" to female heirs. However, it could only be accessed through "interest on the investment during her lifetime, but the principal was to revert after her death to other heirs; it was not to leave the lineage. During her lifetime, both dowry and interest income would be managed by her husband."[16] Catherine King, however, has shown in her work *Renaissance Women Patrons: Wives and Widows in Italy c. 1300-1550* where a small number of women in Italy like Sibilio Cetto and Donna Agnesina did in fact use their family inheritance and became patrons of architecture like their

Ottoman counterparts, although at a much smaller scale. In this position a woman was placed in a commanding role by the will of her father. Like the Ottoman royal women who first had to gain sultanic permission for the building of their mosque complexes, the wives of Renaissance Italy, as Catherine King states, "needed the consent and the administration of their husbands of their dowry and any inheritance [...]"[17] In contrast to the Ottoman royal women who had control of her patronage, for the women of Renaissance of Italy, the husband "acted for the wife [...] about her role in any artistic expression."[18] The wives could in turn use their dowries to fund works of art and architecture, since these gifts were exempt from the fines placed on the rest of the estate. Such workings were vastly different to the complete control that Ottoman women could exercise over their finances; if she had money, she could invest it "via the partnership contracts known as *mudaraba*, which involved [a] silent partner entrusting her money to a travelling merchant".[19]

Patronage of wives and nuns of Renaissance Italy

One of the most impressive examples of charitable expenditure by a woman in Renaissance Italy is the hospital, church and monastery in early 15th century Padua commissioned by the heiress Donna Sibilia Cetto and her husband Ser Baldo Bonafari. Similarly, Donna Agnesina, the wife of Don Girolamo Giustinian, in 1508, saw the completion of the funerary chapel of her father, Don Girolamo Badoer at San Francesco della Vigna in Venice. Unfortunately, the social, religious and legal situations in which Sibilio Cetto and Donna Agnesina participated in the commissioning of art and architecture depict them in a rather submissive position. They had to rely on their male counterparts as executors to carry out their wishes, because as Catherine King states, "they were only contributing to schemes organised by others."[20] They could, in their last will, ask for something to be made or built in her honour. For example, a panel in the Uffizi Gallery by Motervarchi depicting the Madonna and child with four saints, at the feet of Saint Anthony could be wife's posthumous work. The panel reads: "This panel made by Tommaso from San Piero of San Marco for the soul of Mona Filippa his wife and her dead, 14[?]3."[21]

While her husband was in exile in Venice, Sibilia Cetto in Padua commissioned the building of her complex. As the legal document records, she was "acting on her own behalf with her husband absent," emphasising that she was acting somewhat autonomously.[22] This project was funded entirely through Sibilia Cetto's wealth, which she acquired from her father and managed by her husband between 1414 until his death in 1418. The triangular complex situated in the centre of the town also comprised of houses belonging to her signifying her wealth and status. In 1421, now as a widow, she built the church and the convent of San Francesco with the hospital linking the courts of men and women. The colonnaded wing of the south aisle and apse of the church borders the male and female quarters of the church. The portico, planned by Sibilia and Baldo, are supported on columns that run across the facades of the hospital, church and convent expressing their harmony as one project (*Figure 1*).

Figure 1. Hospital / convent of Sibilia Cetto in Padua. Photograph by Metin Mustafa, October, 1999.

Architecturally speaking, this signifies her equal status in the commissioning of this work and philanthropic contribution to the Paduan society of the time.

In 1421 Sibilia Cetto commissioned a tomb for herself and her husband signifying their social status in Padua. While Baldo is dressed depicting his profession as a lawyer, interestingly Sibilia is seen wearing "the corded robe of a Franciscan nun, which she had asked to be buried wearing"[23] (*Figure 2*).

Figure 2. Tomb of Badua and Sibilia. Photograph by Metin Mustafa, October, 1999.

Like the Ottoman royal women depicting themselves as "Mothers of the Believers" through their artistic representations and philanthropic works connecting them with the women of Prophet Muhammad, here, the Paduan lady wearing the garb of a Franciscan nun conveys a similar socio-religious message of purity and piety. Interestingly as Iris Origo notes, by putting her husband beside her in the tomb she demonstrates her reliance on the status of the male to acknowledge her as a great benefactress.[24]

Meanwhile the purpose in commissioning the funerary chapel of Donna Agnesina had more to do with not only honouring her family but also herself as a patron of the arts. As a daughter of a Venetian magistrate, Girolamo Badoer, Agnesina followed in her father's footsteps in terms of sculptural patronage. According to King, he "[h]aving ordered reliefs of a Madonna and Child and Saint Jerome for the tombs of his father and uncle in San Francesco della Vigna, and also, with fellow-magistrates, commissioned the Madonna della Biade for the Palazzo Ducale."[25] Like Sibilia Cetto, Agnesina inherited her father's fortune at his death in 1495. While commissioning of family funerary chapels were mainly carried out by the head of the household, Agnesina, resorts to mimicry through an undertaking of such a task, while her husband is in exile, to assert her identity within the family context. Agnesina's mother, Donna Michaela acknowledges "[t]he tomb which has been made at San Francesco della Vigna by my husband Don Girolamo"[26] while his will instructs "my most beloved Agnesina"[27] to make a marble altarpiece with "Saint Antony in the middle wearing the habit of Saint Francis. Saints Jerome and Michael next on the sides. Saint Agnes [and] Saint Benedict next. The Madonna above. And let it be made beautiful, and do not consider the expense."[28]

Agnesina had the iconographical scheme modified after her second marriage to Girolamo Giustinian. As the central figure she had substituted Saint Jerome for Anthony in the centre, thereby honouring her second husband and her father together. Remaining with the allusions to Saint Jerome she had the *predella* depicted with scenes from the saint's life. Next, Agnesina removed Saint Benedict completely from the visual repertoire because he was the patron saint of her deceased first husband and placed a Madonna in the upper part of the altarpiece. In this funerary chapel it becomes obvious that this female patron celebrated both her father and her new husband and revelled in her own independence (*Figure 3*).

Saint James was now added to the right of Jerome, possibly to honour the patron saint of her paternal great-grandfather, Giacomo. Saint Agnes and Michael were taken over her father's original plan; since they were referred to the patron saints of Agnesina and her mother Donna Michaela, they were given the places of honour to the left.[29]

Figure 3. The altar of the funerary chapel of Badoer family commissioned by Donna Agnesina. Saint Jerome is seen in the centre with St. Agnes and St. Michael on the left; the sculptor Pietro Lombardo depicts St. James and St. Anthony on the right. Photograph by M. Aksoy, June, 2011.

By manipulating the visual symbolisms of the interior of the chapel to suit her present identity, Agnesina was merely asserting her authority as an independent patron of the arts and thus challenging the patriarchal restrictions placed on her representation of 'self'.

To further celebrate this family unity Agnesina had two inscriptions placed at the chapel after the death of her second husband in 1532. While the left inscription is dedicated to her father and her uncle; the right is dedicated to her husband calling him a "like-minded husband", in order to signify that he was in agreement with her actions.[30] Meanwhile, in the visual representations of this joint husband-wife venture it was customary during the Renaissance to represent the woman's heraldry to the right and the man's to the left. However, as a woman, oscillating between the 'self' and her allegiance to her father, Agnesina instead reversed the positions of the arms of her paternal family in the place of honour instead of her husband's. In doing so, she claimed the funerary chapel for the Badoer family. By subverting these patriarchal conventions of the time, and reinforcing her actions of mimicry, Agnesina asserted her authority as an independent patron of the arts by manipulating the social norms to, once again, suit her identity. Although this chapel symbolised a private family space, its popularity with the public, however, cemented her role as a patron and daughter of one of the Magistrates of the Grains in Venice during the sixteenth century.

Furthermore, Chiara Gambacorta demonstrated her power and authority through the commissioning of the 13th century work commissioned at the convent of San Domenico of Pisa. Specifically, Ann M. Roberts has shown that Gambacorta used her influence in Pisa to promote the cult of Swedish St. Birgitta—with which her life shared many parallels—and held special feast days in San Domenico for public preaching about the saint.[31] Gambacorta and St. Birgitta were both concerned with reforming the church and possessed the gift of compassion. Therefore, according to Roberts, Chiara Gambacorta's devotion was her deliberate exertion of power because the saint's presence in the predella, which was destined for the high altarpiece of the church of San Domenico, was not linked to the liturgy of the Sisters' order. The predella of St. Birgitta depicts her writing down the words of an angel, and those that Christ and Virgin Mary dictated to her. Additionally, white roses are shown pouring from her mouth as she saves pilgrims from a shipwreck. From within the context of the spiritual and liturgical life of San Domenico's Sisters, the choice of St. Birgitta makes sense. However, within the main altar of the public church the focus of the predella could only have been on St. Dominic and related saints.[32] Therefore, by emphasising St. Birgitta's writings, visions and miracles, Gambacorta deliberately chose not to include the founder of her order. Rather, in order to promote her veneration, she chose to highlight the aspects of St. Birgitta's life that she felt were more significant to a Pisan audience.

The influence of religious women can also be seen with the artworks commissioned by the nuns of San Zaccaria, for the altarpiece at the chapel of San Tarasio. The inscriptions on the lower left part of the fresco of the main altarpiece show that Abbess Elena Foscari and Prioress Marina Donato commissioned the work. This exemplifies the impact of Renaissance religious women's patronage. Furthermore, representing themselves through the saints of their namesake augmented their authority in male-free environments. St. Elena in the San Tarasio fresco, "represented by a wooden matron holding a cross on the far right of the front of the main altar"[33] stands for Abbess Elena Foscari, while St. Marina—who joined the convent dressed as a man and "was only discovered to be a woman after her death"[34]—represents the Prioress Marina Donato. Therefore, not only did such women express their power and authority through commissioned works of art, they also did so by choosing how, and the saints through which, they asserted their identities. Therefore, what can be deduced by the commissioning of such works is the continuing historical debate concerning the manner in which these Renaissance women through their artistic contributions asserted their presence in a predominantly patriarchal social order.

Patronage of Ottoman imperial women of Renaissance Istanbul

Similarly, the representations of Ottoman women in Renaissance Istanbul[35] are evident in the language of *harem* architecture and aesthetics. This is significant when attempting to deconstruct the ever-growing presence and power of the mother of the sultan. Symbolically, the architecture of Topkapı Palace reflects the power status of the *valide sultan*. In fact, the complete unification of the residence of the sultan and his family occurred under Murad III (1574-95). It was also during his reign that the *harem*, through the work of Sinan, was enlarged; almost rebuilt and took its present-day form. The structural formation, the institutionalisation and the hierarchical formation of the *harem* were also completed during this period.[36] In the Imperial Harem the living quarters of the royal family are defined by the centrality of their locations, in which the rooms connected to all parts of the *harem* sectors, the *valide sultan's* room included a direct link to her son's quarters *(Figures 4, 5)*. This aesthetic could not have been achieved without her presence in the compound. This signifies the importance of the son-mother rule, and the rise of the female sovereign. Therefore, it is no coincidence that Sultan Murad III moved his private quarters from the third courtyard into the *harem*. Thus, the presence of women in the *harem* influenced its physical layout, and its layout reflected their power and authority. Until the reign of Murad III only the sultan accessed the room with the grilled window, which Mehmed II had built a century and a half earlier, to secretly listen in on his Divan Council ministers when he did not wish to attend meetings (*Figure 6*).

Figures 4, 5. Left and right, corridor connecting the prince's chamber to his mother's, built by Sinan. The architecture symbolises the political connection and the power of the Valide Sultan. Photographs by Metin Mustafa, December 2014.

Figure 6. Window with lattice situated beneath the Tower of Justice, the Divan Council of the Topkapı Palace. View from the Harem. Photograph by Metin Mustafa, December, 2014.

Later sultans also followed this protocol, but eventually, the *valide sultan* was also granted access to the room, on behalf of her son, in order to make necessary decisions and determine which of the ministers would be most useful to form political alliances with and who would ensure her safety, as well as that of her son. At this stage, it is apparent that Ottoman royal women had begun to assert their 'presence of absence'; symbolised by the lattice window on the inside, which looks into the male domain, demonstrates their "presence of absence". Additionally, they were able to use gendered spaces and spatial politics for her own political transformation.[37] In such space, the *valide sultan's* act of listening to news from Buda to Yemen, Baghdad to Cairo, and Crimea to Algiers, allowed her to subvert patriarchal norms and became a woman of her own making. She was also making symbolic claims to her political rights, and survival; between 'being' and 'non-being'. That is, she was no longer a slave or servant of the sultan, but co-ruler of the Empire, which required her wit and cunning. For example, the Venetian bailo, Cristoforo Valier, wrote that Kösem Sultan "can do what she wishes with the King and possesses his heart absolutely, nor is anything ever denied to her."[38]

Using the vast individual fortunes Ottoman royal women had at their disposal, they made contributions to public welfare, such as endowing religious foundations and freeing slaves. Ottoman imperial women, through their patronage of large complexes, also provided charity aimed at helping other women, orphans and prostitutes. Charity, as one of the pillars of Islam, is incumbent on Muslims with means, and such work is clearly evident in the Haseki complex of Hürrem Sultan, Mihrimah Sultan and Nurbanu Sultan, and her daughters Ismihan Sultan and Shahsultan. According to Pierce, Ottoman "women asserted the prerogative of claiming and organizing a sector of public life of their own welfare".[39] Similarly, in Ann Matter's study of the commentary on the rule of St. Clare of Assisi—by the 17th century Capuchin nun, Maria Domitilla Galluzzi—Matter suggests there was a "certain trade-off where the convent represented for no man – although strict monastic enclosure and discipline exacted a price, a woman had an opportunity and a context for self-expression which she would not have had otherwise."[40]

Just as the early Renaissance nuns, like Chiara Gambacorta, were renowned for their charity, piety, good counsel and leadership, the paintings of *Siyer-i Nebi*, which was commissioned by Murad III, allude to Ottoman royal women in a similar light.[41] The manuscript also highlights a symbolic connection between Muhammad's mother, Amina, and the *valide* sultan. Similarly, the Prophet's wives can be seen to represent the wives of the sultan, and Muhammad's daughter, Fatima, as the ideal daughter. Ottoman imperial women, like Hürrem Sultan and Nurbanu Sultan, have been compared to the "Mothers of the Believers", which is a term used in the Qur'an to describe the wives of the Prophet.[42] Their 'sacred' status as 'mothers of the believers' also connected them to the Prophet Muhammad's 'ideal' Muslim women—for example, his wives, Khadija and Aisha, and his daughter, Fatima—and may explain why they were largely prohibited from being visually depicted in paintings or seen in public.[43] However, this religious argument becomes problematic, and even contradictory, when works such as *Siyer-i Nebi*, clearly depict the women from Muhammad's life, in miniatures, albeit without their faces on display (*Figure 7*).

Figure 7. Muhammad and Aisha freeing a slave, Siyer-i Nebi, Istanbul, 1595. Photograph reproduction.

Through the appropriation of events from the seventh century, during Prophet Muhammad's life, the paintings of the sixteenth century *Siyer-i Nebi* manuscript allude to the roles of Ottoman imperial women, and their agency in public and private spaces.

The Prophet's wives, mother, and daughter, were the ideal women for Muslim women to emulate. From this perspective the same can be said for Mihrimah and Nurbanu Sultans, and other women of the Ottoman court who, through their pious work, embodied the seventh-century ideal. Indeed, in her *vakfiya* of 1550, the princess Mihrimah is referred to as the sultan's favourite daughter; she is called "Mihrimah Sultan Hanım" and likened to "Fatima in innocence, a Khadija in chastity, an Aisha in intelligence [...] and the Rabi'a of the epoch."[44] These comparisons to the Prophet's family are obvious and reinforce the importance of the piety of

Ottoman women, which, for example, enabled women such as Hürrem to "bring forth on the hidden virtues from behind a veiled canopy, in order that they may be known".[45] Importantly, the *vakfiyes* were composed by men to represent the 'ideal' Muslim woman, as exemplified by the Qur'an and the women of the Prophet's household; however, the paintings present a different portrayal of what may have existed in Ottoman society. In other words, while the *vakfiyes* suggest that it was through their piety that Ottoman royal women wished to be known, as signified by their mosques and upholding of Islamic duties, another version of their lives is just as relevant. After all, these women "behind a veiled canopy"—just like the nuns of San Zaccaria and their renovations to the church of San Tarasio, in 1455—challenged the patriarchy and asserted their authority by demonstrating that it was also their right, as ordained by God, to accomplish deeds like their male counterparts, and thereby, inform the public of their presence. This does not suggest that their intentions were not a result of their Faith, but rather that they were not driven by Faith alone.

Mihrimah Sultan: "Hanım Sultan"

From the security of the Ottoman Imperial *Harem*, the women of the sultan's court embarked on building projects to change the skyline of the imperial city of Renaissance Istanbul. With enormous wealth at their disposal, they became great patrons of architecture, and built many of the mosques, hospitals, bath-houses and fountains that still dominate Istanbul today. Philanthropy also played a major role in the building of these structures, and reinforced their image as ideal Muslim woman.

European fascination with the family of Süleyman is evident in the Florentine artist, Cristofano dell'Altissimo's, portrait copy of Titian's original work (c.1552-1557) of princess Mihrimah, which was produced for Cosimo de'Medici. Princess Mihrimah, whose name means 'sun and moon', was the most privileged (and perhaps most popular) lady of the Ottoman court (*Figure 8*). In the portrait she is shown in traditional Ottoman-Turkish attire and headdress, which Vasari and Ridolfi recorded as having seen, reflect the fashion of the Ottoman Imperial court.

Figure 8. Portrait of Mihrimah Sultan, daughter of Süleyman the Magnificent and Hürrem Sultan, by the Florentine artist Cristofano dell'Altissimo 1552? 1557? for Cosimo de Medici. "Dressed in a plain brown gown with floral motifs, the figure wears a tall headdress ornate with expensive stones. She is set against a dark background upon which are the following inscriptions on the upper left and upper right corners, respectively: 'Cameria Solimani Imparator Filia' (Cameria, Daughter of Sultan Süleyman) and 'Rostanis Bassae Vxor 1541' (Wife of Rüstem Pasha, 1541). It is highly probable that the date inscribed here does not indicate the date on which the work was executed. It can be assumed that the date and the inscription found on virtually all of the similar portraits by different artists repeat a tradition initiated by the first original portrait." Pera Museum, Istanbul, Turkey. Photograph reproduction.

However, European representation of the Süleymanic image, outside Istanbul, added to the curiosity with which Western artists saw the Ottoman court. Currently on display at the Uffizi Gallery, the portrait of Mihrimah Sultan has been identified in the records of 1557 Florence to be dated somewhere between 1552 and 1557.

Sinan built one of the mosque complexes for Mihrimah Sultan during her twenties, while she was the loving and only daughter of Süleyman. However, the second mosque was built for Mihrimah when she had become a widowed princess and was the not-so-beloved sister of Selim II, due to her support for her other brother, Beyazid, to take the throne. Her enormous wealth was doubled by the death of her husband, Rustem Pasha, who left her an annual income of 30 million *aspers*, which gave her a daily stipend of 600 *aspers* and was "the highest sum awarded to any princess in the classical age."[46] Mihrimah Sultan also became the only royal woman to have two mosques built in her name: one at Üsküdar on the shoreline of the Bosphorus with two minarets (as she was permitted to have because she was a royal princess), and the other at Edirnekapı near the Edirne Gate on the city walls, in fact, on the very opposite side of the city from Üsküdar and in the European quarter. This patronage shows her unique status in Süleyman's family (*Figures 9-10*).

Figures 9-10. Above, view from the Bosphorus of the Üsküdar Mosque of Mihrimah Sultan; below, Edirnekapı Mosque of Mihrimah Sultan. Photographs by Metin Mustafa, January, 2015.

Located on the Asian side of the Bosphorus, Üsküdar was on the outside of the political and administrative centre of sixteenth-century Istanbul. However, the town had an active trade route that passed through Asia Minor and on to the Caucasus and Iran. The town was also the starting point of the hajj pilgrimage journey, where every year, pilgrims were sent to Mecca with ceremonies from Üsküdar.[47] Thus, the location was an ideal place to demonstrate Mihrimah's piety to the masses. This first mosque was built near the town's boat landing, between 1543 and 1548. At this location there also sat the garden palace of the princess where she could easily attend prayers, and the inscription panel above the portal of the mosque states that is was built by "Hanım Sultan", (Lady Sultan), the daughter of Süleyman I.[48] The *vakf* records of the complex include a mosque, *madrasah*, guesthouse, caravanserai that also functioned as a stable, elementary school, and an *imaret*, which consisted of a kitchen, pantry and storage area.[49] However, what is of most significance is the location of the mosque and how Sinan used it to represent his princess patron, and perhaps his affection for her. As with so much of his other work, Sinan demonstrates his architectural genius through the complex. While it was a difficult site for construction, as it was an irregular plot of land between the hillside and the Bosphorus shoreline,

Sinan ingeniously planned the mosque in a linear way, and incorporated a second porch in front (instead of using a typical court scheme) as there was not enough space for a court. This design adaptation also acts as an illusion of seclusion for his princess patron, as, when viewed from the front, it cuts out the light from the main entrance.

The architect built the mosque and the *madrasah* on the same horizontal axis, i.e., between the hilltop, behind it, and what was once the Bosphorus shore, in front. He elevated both buildings on a terrace and both can be reached by separate staircases. Additionally, a lane separates the elementary school from the rest of the buildings, and to the east, Sinan built an ablution fountain—between the mosque and the *madrasah*.

The single-domed mosque can be entered from two sides, and is supported by half-domes on all sides, except for the main entrance. The structural connection between the domes and the walls is achieved with pendentives at the central dome and the decorative *muqarnas* by the triumphs at the adjacent half-domes. Sinan used two internal supports to carry the dome rather than the exterior walls (*Figure 11*). As Erzen explains, Sinan did this to focus on the external appearance of the mosque, which was important because of its prominent location.[50] However, as D. Fairchild Ruggles states:

> […] representation is to some degree controlled by the patroness […] Building, painting, sculpting, and writing are always negotiated processes that depend to varying degrees in the patron, the artist, regional and historical techniques and concepts of style, and finally on the audience and its readiness to receive, understand, and legitimate a work of art […].[51]

Therefore, Mihrimah Sultan's position within the royal family, and her close involvement in the building of her husband's mosque, suggest, she have had control over her own mosque's aesthetic appeal.

Figure 11. Front entrance of Üsküdar Mosque. Photograph by Metin Mustafa, January, 2015.

The interior of the mosque, except for the small domed spaces at its corners, demonstrates complete unity. This is highlighted on the mass organisation that can be perceived from the outside. Because the external walls are plain, due to their load bearing elements, the view of the interior of the mosque (from the outside)—featuring its half domes and the unified space beneath them, as well as the portico roof that contributes to a pyramidal effect—reinforces the holistic essence of the design. Goodwin describes the mass of the mosque as "logical", "elegant" and "poetic", and these attributes were made possible by Sinan's manipulation of light and shadow on the mosque exterior[52] (*Figures 12-13*). The gracefulness of the dome and the semi-domes truly provide an effeminate elegance. As part of this mosque, Sinan built three porticos: the first before the main entrance, covered with five domes and supported by lozenge columns; the second surrounding the first portico on three sides, which balances the lack of preliminary space and the sudden entrance into the central domed-space of the mosque, and the third that is a kiosk-like portico over the ablution fountain.

Figures 12-13. Right, interior of the Üsküdar Mosque of Mihrimah Sultan. Below, the elegant domes of the Üsküdar Mosque. Photographs by Metin Mustafa, January, 2015.

This traditional Byzantine element, which Sinan introduced to the Ottoman Empire for the first time, signifies an interplay between his past and present, and represents his 'looking back' to a classical age and adapting its aesthetics to meet the requirements of the Islamic tradition in his contemporary world. The three porticos leading to the single-domed interior give the viewer a delicate impression. From an aerial view of the mosque it can be seen that Sinan shaped the outline of the mosque to look like a woman sweeping the floors that lead to the Bosphorus. At sunset, another woman's outline can be seen when approaching the mosque from the Bosphorus—the fading light produces a silhouette of a woman in a skirt. The Bosphorus location of the mosque also reflects earlier versions of shore pavilions and kiosks that belonged to Ottoman Princesses.[53] The mosque on the waterway is meant to be seen from both the Bosphorus and the European sides of the city.

The mosque complex was not only built for purposes of charity but also to be a very visible representation of Mihrimah Sultan. The architectural theatre that Sinan created in the organisation of the complex, i.e., by placing its main buildings in a linear fashion up near the shore —as opposed to the smaller buildings of the *imaret*, caravanserai and elementary school, that were hidden further back—also demonstrates his patrons desire to have her complex seen as a 'monumental project on stage'. Additionally, the Mihrimah Sultan Mosque in Üsküdar, located away from the political centre of the capital, served many traders and travellers. The functionality of its buildings, and its location at the cross routes of Asia and Europe, demonstrate Sinan's urban planning skills.

The second mosque complex belonging to Mihrimah Sultan, the mosque at Edirnekapı (Edirne Gate), was another major work. Amongst other things, it served the victorious Sultans upon their return to the city from battles outside its walls. It is also in the design and construction of this mosque that Sinan, for the first time, triumphantly used light as a metaphor to create an artistic expression; through the use of a single dome for the Edirnekapı structure. In terms of its size and aesthetic refinement, this mosque eclipsed Mihrimah's earlier mosque at Üsküdar. Symbolically, the Edirnekapı Mosque expressed her image as a wealthy and influential widow—to whom her father, Suleyman, after Hürrem's death, turned to for advice during the final years of his life. Another reading of this mosque complex is that with both her mother and husband deceased, Mihrimah was finally able to shine in her own light, and did so through the commission of this work. In August 1563, Süleyman issued a permit that allowed his daughter to build a mosque at the Edirne Gate location:

> My daughter, may her honour be perpetual, was previously given an august permit from my lofty court to build a noble Friday mosque and a carvansaray free of charge at the protected metropolis of Istanbul inside the Edirne gate.[54]

The planning of Mihrimah's Edirne Gate mosque was completed at the height of Sinan's artistic creativity. In his creation of this mosque, Sinan also moved away from using a cascade of domes that can be seen in the mosques of Mihrimah's father and brothers. According to Susan Skilliter—unlike Sinan's domes from the Süleymaniye mosque—at Istanbul, Sinan employed "a continuous shell seamlessly raised in a drum without external props. It emanates organically from the body of the mosque, entirely dominating the lower domes of the portico and the lateral aisles."[55] In fact, in its multiple-domed, pyramidal design it was the largest and highest dome that Sinan had ever built for a royal woman, and it dominated the entire mosque complex.

Additionally, by designing the mosque in such a way, Sinan was able to focus on creating a taller facade by transforming it into, what Necipoğlu describes as, "transparent screens perforated with multiple tiers of windows".[56] By surrounding the circular tambour and the tympanum walls with windows, Sinan was able to contribute to the mosque's impression of weightlessness and flood the interior with light. The architect's use of the structural skeleton of the mosque, as a lattice for illuminating its interior, has been compared to the screen-wall effect of late Gothic architecture. According to Kuban, Sinan's decision to use such an effect demonstrates just how bold an architect he was, and resulted in an "extraordinary curtain wall articulated by windows" that illuminate the interior.[57] The symbolism of the latticed windows also represents his female patron and alludes to her seclusion. However, the many squares within these latticed windows also allowed Sinan to use light to his advantage, i.e., by allowing little bubbles of sunlight to enter and decorate the interior, and metaphorically represent Mihrimah's beauty.

As a royal princess, Mihrimah was permitted (unlike her haseki mother) to build two minarets in her mosques. However, the single minaret at the Edirnekapı Mosque suggest that her brother, Sultan Selim II—in retribution for her support of Bajezid's (her other brother) ascension to the throne—prevented her from building a second minaret. Consequently, the use of a single minaret became the accepted architectural practice for other royal princesses and was incorporated into the designs of the mosques of her nieces, Ismihan Sultan and Shah Sultan.

The use of abundant lighting in the mosque through its windows signifies a connection to Mihrimah's name. Just like the meaning of Mihrimah's name, 'sun and moon', the mosque is designed to maximise light from its 204 windows. Unlike the much darker interior of her father's complex, the Edirne mosque has both a "structural grace and the metaphor of light" and it is through these aspects of design that "Sinan articulated the gendered identity of his royal patron"[58] (*Figure 14*).

Additionally, the absence of half-domes allowed Sinan to accentuate the unitary dome, which—when seen in relation to the possible symbolism of the minaret—heightens the speculation surrounding the architect's true, personal motives. In fact, Turkish architectural historians, such as Kuban and Necipoğlu, have regarded the mosque of Mihrimah Sultan—with its single dome that is flooded with light—as the most revolutionary and imaginative monument of its time, as well as amongst any of Sinan's other mosques.

Figure 14. Interior of the Edirnekapı Mosque. Photograph by Metin Mustafa, January, 2015.

The concept of light used in Mihrimah's Edirnekapı mosque culminated, at a much grander scale, in the Selimiye. Unlike her nieces, Ismihan and Shah Sultan, who jointly commissioned mosques with their husbands, Mihrimah's two complexes reveal her special status as Süleyman's favoured daughter. By consecutively building her Edirnekapi mosque (c.1562-65)[59] and her husband's Rustem Pasha Mosque (1560-61), Mihrimah kept her identity separate for his—

perhaps to illustrate her unhappiness in their marriage. However, doing so also individualised Mihrimah's public image, and therefore, it may be said that her husband's smaller mosque not only represented his subordination to Süleyman, his father-in-law, but also to Mihrimah. Another interpretation of the difference between the mosques of Mihrimah and Rustem, her husband, is that Rustem's smaller mosque ties him to the *devshirme* servant image from his past, while Mihrimah's grander mosque alludes to her being born free, as the legitimate child of two royal parents.

Likewise, Mihrimah's mosques at Üsküdar and Edirnekapı also differ and have, therefore, generated a variety of readings into the meanings of their symbolism. By using a single minaret at the Edirnekapı Mosque and flooding the entire interior with light, to symbolise her beauty—Sinan achieved, as he had previously with the Üsküdar mosque, a theatre of architectural symbolism. The love story connection between the artist and his patron encourages further thought when considering that on the day of Mihrimah's birth, 21 March—during the northern equinox when day and night are of equal length—the sun sets behind the single minaret of the Edirnekapı Mosque. However, also during the northern equinox, the moon rises between the twin minarets of the Üsküdar Mosque. Additionally, the limited use of windows in this mosque also symbolises the moon and create an aesthetic pun about the princess's name. Through these subtle messages in Sinan's architecture, he positioned himself as an aesthetic genius and was able to visibly represent the 'feminine' in both the physical and symbolic presence of Mihrimah's mosques.

Nurbanu Sultan—the Ottomanised Venetian Queen (1525-1583)

The identity of Nurbanu (Lady of Light) is shrouded in mystery and uncertainty, as was the case with many of the *harem's* concubines in the sixteenth century. However, Skilliter believes that Nurbanu was of Venetian origin; suggesting that, in 1537, when the Turkish Admiral, Barbaros Hayreddin, captured 2,000 slaves (during his raid of the Greek Islands) and brought them to Istanbul, Nurbanu was one of the captives. She also suggests that Nurbanu was a slave from the island of Paros, which at the time was under the rule of Venice, and that she may have been the illegitimate daughter of Nicolo Venier (the Venetian Governor of Paros) and a noble woman named Violante Baffo. If Skilliter is correct, Nurbanu's real name would have been Cecilia Venier-Baffo.[60] In fact, in 1559 Nurbanu inquired after the identity of her (supposedly Venetian) parents and sought to confirm that her nearest living relative—her cousin, Zuan Francesco Venier—was from Corfu. Unfortunately, Ambassador Marino Cavalli, who dealt with Nurbanu about the matters, could not substantiate any claims. However, according to the bailo, Paolo Contarini, Nurbanu flaunted her apparent Venetian heritage because she had memories of being born as a "gentile-donna veneziana"[61], and had recollections of her family's palace on the Grand Canal.[62] Another account of Nurbanu's behaviour exists in a complaint made by the French ambassador, in 1583, regarding Nurbanu's partiality for Venetian diplomats and merchants, "as much because it is said that she is from their country as because of the grand and frequent presents they give her".[63] A fact further supported by Pierce, who has shown that during her lifetime Nurbanu received 2,000 sequins for her services to the Venetian Senate, and for preventing Selim II's invasion of Crete.[64]

After Hürrem Sultan, Nurbanu was the only other Haseki to have lawfully married a Sultan. Additionally, after outliving her husband, Selim II, she became the first Ottoman queen mother to receive the title of Valide Sultan. As Pinar Kayaalp notes, "when her son, Murad III became Sultan, Nurbanu officially took on the title of Valide Sultan, or Queen Mother, holding the highest office of the imperial harem until her death in 1583."[65] The foundations of the mosque of Nurbanu Sultan, known as Atik Valide Sultan Mosque, were laid in 1571—the same year she legally married and received a dowry of 110,000 ducats. As the wife of a sultan, Nurbanu also received a daily allowance of 1,000 aspers, while the other women of the harem received only 30 to 40 aspers.[66] Among her many *vakfiye* (charitable endowments), Nurbanu's Atik Valide Mosque was the largest endowment from any female patron at that point in Ottoman history and one that "constitutes the architectural embodiment of Nurbanu's prestige, power and piety."[67] In fact, through both her enormous wealth and power, the restrictions and seclusion that applied to Ottoman women did not hinder her influence. The Valide Sultan's *vakfiyes* are testimony to this. In fact, the epigraph in her mosque mentions no name other than Nurbanu's, which suggests that she was independent of any male patron.[68] However, she was very close to her son, Murad III, and in her funeral procession miniature painting by Lokman, he is shown walking alongside her coffin and openly weeping (*Figure 14a*). The miniature is also a record of what was one of the most significant events in Ottoman royal history, due to its depiction of the lavish public ceremonies that were held in Nurbanu's honour, both in life and death.

Figure 14a. A miniature painting by Lokman depicting the funeral procession of Nurbanu Sultan, c.1581. Photograph reproduction.

Additionally, her burial was the first time an Ottoman royal woman had been allowed to rest in the same tomb as her Sultan husband, and according to the wishes of her son, Nurbanu's body was placed on a raised platform to indicate that her status was equal to the late Sultan's (*Figure 15*).

Figure 15. The sarcophagi of Selim II (left) and his wife Nurbanu Sultan (right). Photograph by Metin Mustafa, January, 2015.

The building of Imperial Friday mosque complexes, in the capital of the Empire, began with Murad I in the fourteenth century at Bursa. This tradition continued through to Suleyman the Magnificent, but his son, Selim II—unable to match his father's grandiosity, personal dominance or skills—broke with this tradition and built the Selimiye in Edirne. Later, his son, Murad III, also built in the province of Manisa, which was the location of his princely governorate. Therefore, the capital was now left to women, who adorned it through their patronage, which was symbolic of who was 'really in charge' at the palace. With Nurbanu Sultan assuming a sultanic right through the building of her mosque in Istanbul[69], at the same time as her husband's complex in Edirne, demonstrates another step toward the integration of imperial women into public expressions of dynastic sovereignty.

Building an imperial mosque in the capital represented more authority than Selim II's inability to match his father's majestic mosque, the Süleymaniye in Istanbul. Instead, he settled to build his imperial complex in Edirne. Therefore, Nurbanu Sultan, through her architecture in Istanbul—on the Asian side of the Bosphorus and facing the Süleymaniye—surpassed her husband in reputation, and bolstered her authority as an Ottoman royal woman by achieving something that Selim II could not.

The Valide Sultan's *vakfiye*, of April 1583, names her as the patroness of architecture. The Turkish inscription on the wooden panel, above the *muqarnas* of the white marble gate of the double portico reads:

> This peerless work of charity is her personal foundation; Its date was 'Excellent, sublime paradise!' 991 (1583-84)[70]

Having outlived her husband, Selim II, by nine years, the widow queen's mosque at Üsküdar (further inland from the Bosphorus than Mihrimah's mosque), came to be known as the Atik Valide Mosque (that is the Old Queen Mother's Mosque). The construction of Nurbanu's grand mosque began in c.1570-71 and was continued, after her death in 1583, by her son Murad III. At the time of building the Atik Valide Mosque, Sinan was busy with the construction of the Selimiye (1568-74) complex in Edirne. Therefore, he left the initial building stages of Nurbanu's mosque to his assistant.

The building of the mosque was divided into three stages and coincided with Nurbanu's rise through various positions of power. The first stage, between 1571-74, was when she was the wife of Selim II. The second stage, between 1574 and 1577/78—by which time Sinan had taken over from his assistant—was also when Nurbanu was the Valide Sultan. Therefore, it was during this second phase that Sinan modified the design plans for the mosque and added: a second, single-galleried minaret; an extension of the portico through the addition of an outer porch, and a 12.7 metre dome that to rest on a "hexagonal support system with two free-standing brownish porphyry columns [...] surrounded by four exedral half-domes and a half-domed projecting mihrab".[71] Finally, to represent her ever-growing status, the third stage corresponded with building the expanded version of the complex, which Sinan had planned prior to his departure to Mecca, in 1584. Therefore, the third phase of the project was left in the hands of either Davud Pasha or the chief black eunuch, Mehmed Agha—who was the chief overseer of the mosque's *vakf*. This final stage of construction also aligns with the *Valide's* final years. However, Kuban disagrees that the second stage could not have been built by Sinan, and therefore, the unity of the prayer space was compromised by the columns independent of the two side supporting walls of the hexagon. This work was obviously not due to Sinan, not only because of his absence but because "he could never have thrown aside all his architectural understanding to produce in 1583 an inferior version of the Üç Şerefeli plan he had experimented with in 1555 [in Edirne]."[72] Additionally, the size of the dome and the two porticos, compared to the 20.25 metre dome of Mihrimah Sultan's Edirnekapı Mosque and the three porticos of her Üsküdar Mosque, further raise suspicions about his feelings towards the princess. After all, the largest dome Sinan had ever built for a woman did not belong to the great Valide Sultan, but to Mihrimah Sultan (*Figures 16-18*).

Figures 16-17. Right, portico of the Atik Valide Mosque; below, the double portico of the Atik Valide Mosque. Photographs by Metin Mustafa, January, 2015.

As with his work on Mihrimah's mosques, the location of the Atik Valide Mosque played an important role and allowed Sinan to design a sophisticated, organic, urban complex, using skills that had developed during the latter part of his long career. Therefore, in the Atik Valide Mosque, Sinan discarded the geometric rigidity of the Süleymaniye, Selimiye, and other complexes of the past.

Figure 18. The 12.7 metre dome of the Atik Valide Mosque. Photograph by Metin Mustafa, January, 2015.

With a more informal and lyrical approach to the Atik Valide Mosque, Sinan merged his architecture with the slightly sloping hillside of its location. At the same time, he maintained the hierarchical order of the buildings by placing the *hamam* (bath-house) and the caravanserai at the lowest levels. Above these were placed the hospice and hospital, while the *madrasahs* were left for the uppermost level. By surrounding the garden with domed arcades and iron-grilled windows, Sinan invites the visitor to delight in the panorama of the landscape and his work.[73] As Evliya Çelebi has also noted, Sinan's genius can be seen in the monumental structure of the mosque and the skill with which he used the landscape to the advantage of the mosque:

> Situated on a slope, it is like a dome of light. On its three sides are upper galleries for the congregation and multi-tiered oil lamps; it also has stained glass windows. The mosque features lateral domes and its big central dome is especially lofty. Plane trees and linden trees have been planted in its courtyard. On its right and left sides are two well-proportioned minarets with single galleries. All the buildings are completely covered with resplendent blue lead; they are strongly built monumental structures created by Mimar Sinan.[74]

Using a stairway to connect the mosque to the *madrasah* with the courtyard garden, Sinan created an aesthetic effect that is one of the most important features of Sinan's urban design, and lends itself to its own "peculiar identity".[75]

During the expansion stage, Sinan added U-shaped galleries by creating a crowded feeling in the prayer hall, thereby diminishing the unity of the uninterrupted space he achieved in the Selimiye (*Figure 17*). The galleries vary in level, as the women's prayer section in Ottoman mosques was always in the upper gallery. Therefore, the crowded feeling represented by the balconies may have been Sinan's attempt to represent the presence of women in a more obvious way, and therefore, provide more of a gender balance among the worshippers. The 'U' shape that Sinan used at the *qibla* wall and decorated with Iznik tiles provides the enclosed sanctuary feeling of the *harem*, and signifies that this structure was built for an imperial woman. However, the design is not intimidating, but rather, welcoming and embracing—just as Nurbanu had wanted to be remembered by her subjects confirming the Venetian *bailo* Contarini's words, "everybody admits in general that she was an excessively good, courageous and erudite woman"[76] (*Figure 19-20*).

Figures 19, 20. Left, the U-shaped interior; right, the U-shaped qibla wall facing the Queen's balcony. Photographs by Metin Mustafa, January, 2015.

Focusing on the nature of his female patron, Nurbanu, Sinan included a stately balcony with a five-arched colonnade to attract the worshipper to the mosque's anti-*qibla* location. This also allowed his female patron to have an uninterrupted gaze of her male subjects below (*Figures 21-22*). The Queen's balcony, thus, architecturally represents her elevated status as the Queen of the Empire; and her presence at this location during Friday prayers, gazing down on her subjects below would have definitively signified a reversal of gender roles within the ruling echelons of the empire.

Figures 21, 22. Left, the five-arched colonnade balcony allowing Sinan's royal patron uninterrupted gaze of her male subjects below; right, looking at the mimbar and the qibla wall from the royal balcony. Photographs by Metin Mustafa, January, 2015.

Just like Donna Agnesina (mentioned above) reversing the positions of the arms of her paternal family in the place of honour instead of her husband's in order to represent her father and her identity as the patroness; here Nurbanu Sultan's grandiose balcony equally reverses the social conventions of the time, and places herself, both literally and symbolically at the top of the pyramid of the male ruling hierarchy, while her son Murad III is safely ensconced in the harem. By mimicking the male role physically at this focal point of the mosque, this Venetian-Ottoman Queen, thus, symbolically becomes the sole sovereign of the empire. As Kayaalp asserts, "the mosque complex (*külliye*) is indeed an eloquent representation of the identity of the woman behind its actualization, aptly projecting Nurbanu's beneficence and piety simultaneously with her wealth and might."[77] Furthermore, her weekly presence here would have demonstrated her as a pious Muslim woman as the "Mother[s} of Believers" further exalting her place in the eyes of her subjects.[78]

The balcony's flat vault, as seen from the northern exterior above the double portico, includes a triple-windowed rectangular projection (*Figure 23*). The lattice window, therefore, becomes an external symbol of Nurbanu's presence, and there is unlikely to be any explanation for it, other than Sinan including for his female patron. According to the *Hanafi* tradition, young women were not encouraged to attend congregational prayers, but this rule did not apply to widows like Nurbanu.

Figure 23. The lattice windows on the domes. Photograph by Metin Mustafa, January, 2015.

Additionally, as this was a mosque for a woman, Sinan did not include a 'sultan's box' or a private quarter that could be used by the Sultan for worship and reflection, such as those seen in the Süleymaniye and Selimiye mosques. Instead, the 'queen's balcony' may have served similar—albeit, subversive—functions. Therefore, through the metaphor of the balcony (both from the interior and exterior of the mosque), Sinan negated the 'illusion of seclusion'.

Nurbanu Sultan's large complex was only rivalled by the Süleymaniye and the mosque of Mehmed II, in Istanbul. This fact demonstrates just how powerful her position, as a female sovereign in the Ottoman Empire, was during the period. Additionally, Murad III's continued support of his mother's posthumous mosque and *vakf* foundations demonstrate the special bond that existed between this mother and son. Perhaps this is why Murad III did not build his own imperial mosque in the capital, and chose to do so in Manisa; away from his mother's Atik Valide Mosque so that the architectural memorial of this Ottomanised Venetian Queen would be certain to retain its unparalleled greatness.

As indicated above, the Ottoman structures built by Sinan (as well as later architects) make connections between both abstract and physical notions of the 'other' and the actual social situation of Ottoman women. These structures, which still stand today, contradict the *absence* of the female, and their existence/non-existence as 'that which cannot be represented'.[79] Therefore, the positions taken by Irigaray, Coleman, Derrida and Foucault resonate with gendered readings of the mosque complexes of Ottoman imperial women. While modernism has largely excluded women, feminists have re-asserted and celebrated their achievements, in relation to the historical context of their lives. Perhaps the mosques of the sultanas should be perceived as products of an alternative feminine experience; from a different time, culture and people. Additionally, it was important for the Ottoman feminine experience of the sixteenth-century to be recognised by contemporary patriarchal and religious institutions, and through the architectural patronage of Ottoman women we still have architectural evidence of their "presence of absence" and manipulation of gender roles.

Mahpeyker Kösem Sultan (1589-1651)

The women of Ottoman royal society made very efficient use of the visual medium of architecture, particularly its powerful ability to build their 'presence' within mainstream Ottoman society, and their patronage continued well into the seventeenth century. For example, during the height of the 'Sultanate of Women', in the 17th century, Mahpeyker Kösem Sultan[80] commissioned the Çinili Mosque (Tiled Mosque)[81] which mimicked aesthetics that would typically be used by her male counterparts. The mosque's architect, Kasım Agha, decorated its entire interior with Iznik tiles—inspired by Sinan's work for Sultan Süleyman's Grand Vizier in the Rustem Pasha Mosque (1560). The "mimicry" used by the mosque's patron suggests the power of her elevated status as Valide Sultan and the wife of Sultan Ahmet I (d.1617). It also suggests that the assertion of women's authority was still in force almost a century after it had been established by Hürrem Sultan in the sixteenth century.

Mahpeyker Sultan's Çinili Mosque signifies the shift in power at the palace centre, which by this time had become firmly established. After all, not only did she serve as Valide Sultan during the reign of her first son, Murad IV, but she also remained influential when her second son, Ibrahim—who was somewhat mentally unstable—took the throne (1640-48). During Ibrahim's reign it was primarily Mahpeyker Sultan who ruled the Empire on her son's behalf, and she held this extremely influential role through her grandson Mehmed IV's first year of reign in 1648, which was also the year of her passing.

Following in the style of the Rustem Pasha Mosque, the Çinili Mosque predominantly uses cobalt and green tiles, with the addition of large Qur'anic inscriptions on the sidewalls and over the window panels of the *qibla*. These inscriptions serve to balance the Word of God with the symbolism associated with Iznik naturalism, which Sinan had achieved in the Grand Vizier's mosque. However, its minimal use of red in the *mihrab* and border panels, and lack of variety in the design patterns of the tiles, mark the beginning of the decline in Iznik quality and innovation that occurred in the early to mid-seventeenth century. Unlike Sinan's engaging work in the Rustem Pasha Mosque in the previous century, the Çinili Mosque overuses a motif of green carnations and drooping blue tulips on the left and right panels of the *mihrab*, which quickly loses its viewing appeal *(Figures 24-25)* and intensity without the vibrancy of the tomato red that made its debut in the Rustem Pasha Mosque in 1560.

Figures 24, 25. Left, interior of Çinili Mosque of Mahpeyker Kösem, Üsküdar, Istanbul, 1640; right, interior of Rustem Pasha Mosque c. 1560. Photographs by Metin Mustafa, January, 2015.

Sadly, the design of the Çinili Mosque does not achieve the aesthetic excitement created by the Rustem Pasha Mosque or the Atik Valide Mosque. In these two works, Sinan created a vibrant quality within the mosques' interiors and *qibla* walls. Additionally, the use of tiles on the portico of the Atik Valide Mosque—where red floral motifs are interspersed with Qur'anic inscriptions alludes to the female patron of the complex—inspire the viewer. However, the attempt to achieve a similar result in the Çinili Mosque is not nearly as successful. Unfortunately, the decline in Iznik quality—through the loss of vibrant colours and a variety of designs—meant that great works from early in the Süleymanic period could not be replicated or improved (*Figures 26-29*).

Figures 26, 27. Left, tile panel of Çinili Mosque 17th century; right, tile panel of Rustem Pasha Mosque, sixteenth century. Photograph by Metin Mustafa, January, 2015.

Figures 28, 29. Left, mihrab of Çinili Mosque, 1640; right, mihrab wall of Rustem Pasha Mosque, 1560. Photographs by Metin Mustafa, January, 2015.

Legacy of Ottoman Imperial Women

Sinan's legacy has continued in modern Turkey by the country's first mosque to be designed by a woman, Zeynep Fadıllıoğlu. Fadıllıoğlu designed the Şakirin Mosque for women, which opened to worshippers in 2009. Fadıllıoğlu's Şakirin Mosque, like many sixteenth century mosques, was also commissioned by female patrons through the Semiha Şakirin Foundation and is located in Üsküdar, which is also home to Sinan's mosques for Mihrimah Sultan and Nurbanu Sultan (*Figures 30, 31*). In this way, the new mosque represents the continuation of the legacy of the patronage of women.

Figures 30, 31. Left and right, the exterior view of the Şakirin Mosque designed by Turkey's first woman architect Zeynep Fadıllıoğlu, appropriating Sinan's sixteenth century classical style as seen in the image on the right. Photographs by Metin Mustafa, January, 2015.

Zeynep Fadıllıoğlu and her team, mostly made up of women artists, "created a very modern interior and redesigned a totally new concept" by uniting past Turkish traditions from mosques of the sixteenth century—that is, both their decoration and architectural elements—to create something new.[82] Through appropriating Sinan's mosque elements, use of wrought iron windows for corridors and glass facade walls, decorated with gold Qur'anic inscriptions on the inside glass that surround the space, this post-modern mosque is filled with light (*Figure 32*). Furthermore, the architect appropriated the traditional Ottoman tulip motif symbolising Allah[83] into the single piece turquoise *mihrab* with gold inlay protruding out of the *qibla* wall ready to embrace the worshippers (*Figure 32a*).

Figure 32. The interior of the Şakirin Mosque with a view of the tulip shaped turquoise and gold mihrab, and the mimbar. Photograph by Metin Mustafa, January, 2015.

The interior of the niche is interspersed with medallion patterns mimicking Iznik tiles of sixteenth century Ottoman Renaissance mosques (*Figure 32b*).[84] The forceful, and yet, graceful tulip shaped *mihrab* is ready to embrace the worshipper and shower him with God's Light and Mercy alluded to by the gold inlay as seen in Figure 32a. This is reminiscent of the 15th century Timurid painter, Mir Heidar's use of gold colour against a turquoise background in representing Prophet Muhammad enveloped by the Light of God during his *mi'raj* journey at *Sidrat el-munteha* (Lotus Tree of the Utmost End) (*Figure 32c*).[85] Just like the Prophet bowing and surrendering before the Light of God in the painting of Mir Heidar, so too, today's worshipper is enveloped by God's Light as he prostrates before the turquoise and golden *mihrab* of Zeynep Fadıllıoğlu in the Şakirin Mosque, thus submitting to his Creator.

Figures 32a-c. Right, mihrab wall of the Şakirin Mosque, 2009; centre, mihrab of Rustem Pasha Mosque, 1560; below, 15th century miniature painting of Mir Heidar showing Prophet Muhammad prostrating before the Light of God, from Miraj Nameh, 1436-37. Right and centre photographs by Metin Mustafa, January, 2015.

Additionally, Fadıllıoğlu has eliminated gender differentiation by using a single entrance for the mosque, and therefore, subverting the Sinanian use of two entrances (i.e., one for each of the sexes). In doing so, she has allowed both men and women to enjoy the ambience of the main entrance before moving into their respective sacred spaces. Fadıllıoğlu has also eliminated gender differentiation in a way that is similar to Sinan's use of the imperial balcony, in the Atik Valide Mosque. In Fadıllıoğlu's design of a women's balcony, she has created the potential for uninterrupted gaze; where women can view the large, asymmetrical chandelier glass globes (intended to mimic raindrops). These globes allude to Allah's Mercy falling on worshippers like rain, and suggest that both men and women are recipients of His Mercy (*Figure 33*).

Figure 33. The dome of the Şakirin Mosque with chandelier glass globes mimicking raindrops alluding to Allah's Mercy falling on worshippers. Photograph by Metin Mustafa, January, 2015.

The increased area of space for women, within the Şakirin Mosque, also diverts from traditional conventions and, therefore, allocates for more equal prayer space to both sexes. While the Iznik tiles of the past —which would typically adorn the *qibla* wall—are not present in this modern mosque, calligraphic *thuluth* inscriptions have been used to decorate the dome and the pendentives. This decoration reinforces the significance of 'the Word as Art' and is accompanied by the—now famous—Ottoman flower motif, which is represented by the tulip-shaped, turquoise-coloured *mihrab* that the designer describes as "an opening to God."[86] The amalgamation of the past with the modern mosque (above) signifies the continued importance of women in today's Turkish society, and the influence that Ottoman imperial women continue to assert in their shaping of history.

Therefore, these women's experiences (i.e. both Ottoman and Italian) of the Renaissance like their male counterparts make them equal partners in contributing to its making both artistically and architecturally speaking. Without their contributions the period in discussion would not make sense. Additionally, the similarities in which these women exercised their authority and wealth in representing the 'self' cannot be dismissed either. By employing mimesis they have proven the existence of a 'second sex' in its own right.[87] Furthermore, resorting to 'mimicry' these Renaissance women from both sides of the Mediterranean challenged patriarchal conventions allowing them to cement their authoritative roles as active participants in their respective societies.

Bibliography

Armani, Ricci. "The Şakirin Mosque, 15 December, 2012." Accessed August 14, 2015, http://ricci-armani.com/sakirin-mosque-istanbul/

Artan, Tülay. "Boğaziçi'nin Çehresini Değiştiren Soylu Kadınlar ve Sultanefendi Sarayları," *Istanbul Dergisi* III (1992): 106-118.

Coleman, Debra. "Introduction." In *Architecture and Feminism*. Edited by Debra Coleman, Elizabeth Denza, and Carol Henderson, ix-xvi. New York, Princeton Architectural Press, 1996.

Chojnacki, S. *Women and Men in Renaissance Venice: Twelve Essays on Patrician Society.* Baltimore and London: The John Hopkins University Press, 2000.

Cağman, Filiz and Engin Yenal, eds. *Topkapı: The Palace of Felicity,* trans. Robert Bragner. Istanbul: Ertuğ & Kölük, 1992.

Çelebi, Evliya. *Seyahatname* vol. 1. Istanbul: Devlet Basımevi 1896-1938.

Düzbakar, Ömer. "Charitable Women And Their Pious Foundations In The Ottoman Empire: The Hospital of the Senior Mother, Nurbanu Valide Sultan." Bursa: Uludağ University, Faculty of Arts and Sciences, Department of History, 2006.

Erzen, Jale. *Sinan: Ottoman Architect, an Aesthetic Analysis*. Ankara: Middle East Technical University, Faculty of Architecture, 2004.

Encyclopedia of Islam: New Edition Vol. 8. New York: Brill, 1998.

Efendi, Esad. *Osmanlılarda Töre ve Törenler*, ed. Yavuz Ercan. Istanbul: Baki, 1979.

Faroqhi, Suraiya. *Subjects of the Sultan: Culture and Daily Life in the Ottoman Empire*. London, UK: IB Tauris, 2010.

Freely, John. *Inside the Seraglio: Private Lives of the Sultans in Istanbul*. England: Viking, 1999.

Goodwin, Godfrey. *A History of Ottoman Architecture*. London, UK: Thames and Hudson, 1971.

Kayaalp, Pınar. *The Empress Nurbanu and Ottoman Politics in the Sixteenth Century: Building the Atık Valide*. New York: Routledge, 2018.

Grosz, Elizabeth. "Women, *Chora*, Dwelling," in *Postmodern Cities and Spaces*. Edited by Sophie Watson and Katherine Gibson. Oxford, Blackwell Publishers, 1995.

Irigaray, Luce. *The Sex Which Is Not*. Translated by Catherine Porter and Caroline Burke. Ithaca, New York: Cornell University Press, 1985.

Kayaalp, Pınar. "Vakfiye and Inscriptions: An Interpretation of the Written Records of the Atik Valide Mosque Complex." *International Journal of Islamic Architecture* vol. 1, 2 (2012): 301-324. Accessed September, 23, 2015. http://dx.doi.org/10.1386/ijia.1.2.300_1.

King, Catherine. *Renaissance Women Patrons: Wives and Widows in Italy c. 1300-1550*. UK: Manchester University Press, 1998.

King, Margaret. *Women of the Renaissance*. Chicago: University of Chicago Press, 1991.

Konyalı, Hakkı. *Mimar Koca Sinan'ın Eserleri.* Istanbul: Ülkü Basımevi, 1950.

Kuban, Doğan. *Istanbul Yazıları* Istanbul: Yapı Endustrisi Merkezi Yayınları, 1998.

Kuban, Doğan. *Ottoman Architecture.* Suffolk, UK: Antique Collectors Club Distributors, 2010.

Mazlum, Deniz. *Dünden Bügüne Istanbul Ansiklopedisi*, vol. 7. Istanbul: Kültür Bakanlığı ve Tarih Vakfı Yurt Yayınları Ortak Yayını, 1994.

McIver, Katherine A. *The Sixteenth Century Journal* 27, 2 (1996): 628. Review of *Creative Women in Medieval and Early Modern Italy: A Religious and Artistic Renaissance*, ed. E.A. Matter and J. Coakley (Philadelphia: University of Philadelphia Press), Book Review, DOI: 10.2307/2544244.

Mustafa, Metin. *The Ottoman Renaissance: A Reconsideration of Early Modern Ottoman Art, 1413-1575.* New Jersey: Blue Dome Press, 2019.

Necipoğlu, Gülru. *The Age of Sinan: Architectural Culture in the Ottoman Empire.* London: Reaktion Books, 2005.

Origo, Iris. *The Merchant of Prato: Francesco di Marco Datini.* London: Jonathan Cape, 1957.

Peirce, Leslie P. "Gender and Sexual Propriety in Ottoman Royal Women's Patronage." In *Women, Patronage and Self-Representation in Islamic Societies*, edited by D. Fairchild Ruggles, 53-68. New York: State University of New York Press, 2000.

Peirce, Leslie. *The Imperial Harem: Women and Sovereignty in the Ottoman Empire.* New York: Oxford University Press, 1993.

Qur'an.

Radke, G. "Nuns and their Art: The Case of San Zaccaria in Renaissance Venice." *Renaissance Quarterly*, 54 (2001): 430-459.

Rizani, Zehra. "The Woman Behind the Sakirin Mosque" in *Altmuslimah*, last modified May 27, 2009. Accessed August 14, 2015. http://www.altmuslimah.com/b/mca/3090.

Power, Carla. "Updating the Mosque for the 21st Century." *TIME Magazine*, April, 2, 2009.

Roberts, A. M. "Chiara Gambacorta of Pisa as Patroness of the Arts." In *Creative Women in Medieval and Early Modern Italy*, ed. E.A. Matter and J. Coakley, 120-154. Philadelphia: University of Philadelphia Press.

Ruggles, D. Fairchild. "Vision and Power." In *Women, Patronage and Self-Representation in Islamic Societies*, edited by D. Fairchild Ruggles, 1-16. New York: State University of New York Press, 2000.

Sancar, Aslı. *Ottoman Women, Ottoman Women: Myth and Reality*. New Jersey: The Light, Inc., 2007.

Shick, Irvin Cemil. "The Harem as Gendered Space and the Spatial Reproduction of Gender." In *Harem Histories: Envisioning Places and Living Spaces*, ed. Marilyn Booth. London: Duke University Press, 2010.

Skilliter, Susan. "The Letters of the Venetian 'Sultana' Nur Banu and Her *Kira to Venice*." In *Studia Turcologica Memoriae Alexii Bombaci Dicata*, edited by Gallotta and U. Marazzi, 515-536. Naples: Herder, 1982.

Skilliter, Susan A. "Three Letters from the Ottoman 'Sultana' Safiye to Queen Elizabeth I." *Oriental Studies 3* (1965): 119-57.

Stephan, St. H. "An Endowment Deed of Haseki Sultan, Dated the 24th May, 1552." *Quarterly of the Department of Antiquities in Palestine*, 10 (1994): 170-94.

Thys-Senocak, Lucienne. "The Yeni Valide Mosque Complex of Eminönü, Istanbul (1597-1665): Gender and Vision in Ottoman Architecture." In *Women, Patronage and Self-Representation in Islamic Societies*, edited by D. Fairchild Ruggles, 69-90. New York: State University of New York Press, 2000.

Negotiating Gender in the Early Modern Period - The illusion of seclusion and the metaphors of Ottoman imperial women's sovereignty

ESSAY II

Abstract: Historically, early modern Ottoman imperial women's architectural works have been well documented to demonstrate their sovereignty and authority. Recent scholarship, however, has turned to the nature of gendered architectural necessities and ceremonial processions of early modern Ottoman imperial women to assert their sovereignty to their subjects by their physical presence. By resorting to mimicry, the women of the Ottoman Imperial *Harem* subvert the patriarchal norms of the period. It is the aim of this article to provide another viewpoint from a feminist paradigm to the nature of the sovereignty of the early modern Ottoman imperial women through the visual representations of processional ceremonies and the 1582 illustrated manuscript *Surname-i Hümayun*. Furthermore, by comparing Ottoman imperial women's processional and funeral ceremonies with that of Elizabethan England, there arise similar practices by Renaissance women asserting their power and sovereignty.

Keywords: *sovereignty, harem, imperial, Ottoman Empire, Valide Sultan, processions*

Much has been written on Ottoman imperial women's architectural patronage and philanthropic works in the sixteenth century.[1] While the attention in these works also focused on the gendered mosque architecture to represent the patronage of the imperial women, this article, through the illustrated manuscript *Surname-i Hümayun* (1582) takes a look at a different gendered architectural requirement – pavilions, to propagate the physical presence of these women to their subjects, up close and personal. In addition to informing historians about Ottoman art and daily life in the sixteenth century, the manuscript, *Surname-i Hümayun* underscores the active roles of imperial women in early modern Ottoman ceremonial celebrations. In its depiction of Şehzade (prince) Mehmed's circumcision, which began in the Old Palace near Bajezid II Square in Istanbul, the attendees are said to have included Sultan Murad III (d. 1595) as well as female guests from the Imperial *Harem*. However, unlike the Sultan and Prince's procession, the manuscript does not display the procession of imperial women as they were constrained to observe the ceremonies from the lattice windows of the palace of Ibrahim Pasha and pavilions constructed specifically for women, which overlook At Meydani (the old Roman Hippodrome). This private viewing space of the imperial women including the most important women of the *harem*, the *Valide* Sultan (Queen Mother) and the mother of the prince, demonstrates their "presence of absence", as noted by the feminist historian Eisenman.[2] The lavish processions are equally notable with their Elizabethan counterpart – Elizabeth I. A comparison of the Ottoman and Elizabethan imperial women's procession reveal similar gendered dynamics asserting contemporary Renaissance women's sovereignty. Firstly, the article aims to explore these similarities between the two royal households. Secondly, the aim of the article is to articulate the illusion of seclusion of the early modern Ottoman imperial women, their power, authority and legitimacy of sovereignty, as depicted in the 1582 manuscript – *Surname-i Hümayun*. The visual depictions by the palace artists provide art and cultural historians a different way of looking at the role of royal women in sixteenth century Ottoman society.

Feminist Methodology

Although gender studies have been largely the domain of recent scholarship, there is no intellectual reason as to why such methodological approaches should be limited to the contemporary period. Applying feminist approaches to Ottoman visual studies with respect to self-representation of women in the sixteenth century are important in determining the role early modern Ottoman royal women played in political and social affairs of the empire. According to Islamic practices of the early modern Ottoman court, royal women were "neither expected nor allowed to present their physical selves, unveiled, before the gaze of their subjects."[3] However, gendered architectural spaces allowed the imperial women to be seen in public. Through the "restructuring of space" the architect was able to create gendered space that resulted in spatial politics and historical transformation.[4] Through gendered architectural spaces, the imperial women could obtain and exercise significant control within and outside the traditional space (*haremlik* / private) they inhabited, which they had also often created and endowed.[5]

French feminist-philosopher, Luce Irigaray states that in order for women from history to assign to the feminine they had to resort to "mimicry", and convert "a form of subordination into an affirmation, and thus to begin to thwart it."[6] According to Irigaray, women demand to speak as a masculine "subject", and through mimesis, a woman attempts to recover her place from exploitation by discourse: "without allowing herself to be simply reduced to it. It means to resubmit herself – inasmuch as she is on the side of the "perceptible" of "matter" – to "ideas" in particular to ideas about herself, that are elaborated in/by a masculine logic."[7] By applying this *universal* interpretation to Ottoman imperial woman of the sixteenth and seventeenth centuries, they demonstrate their subversion of the Ottoman social order, and negate being "products" for use and exchange by men.[8] Furthermore, through this demonstration of masculine mimesis, "even though she is hidden, most often hidden as woman and absent in the capacity of subject, manages to make 'sense' […] manages to create 'content'."[9] Therefore, when gendered architecture is used as a metaphor, the illusion of seclusion changes to a representation of reality, that is, of the sovereignty of Ottoman royal women.

In the introduction to *Architecture and Feminism*, Deborah Coleman asks, "[w]hat role does architectural discourse itself play in preserving gender-based relations of power?"[10] The difficulty, she stresses, in attempting to answer this is to risk revealing the complicity of architectural discourse in the struggles over the mobility and social space granted to women.[11] Indeed, the limited social space granted to Ottoman imperial women is crucial to fully understanding their patronage and assertion of power. Similarly, interpreting Plato and Jacques Derrida, in her essay titled "Women, Chora, Dwelling", Elizabeth Grosz states that Plato's featureless, neutral, but altogether necessary "bridge" between the world of Forms or Ideas and material reality can be understood as the basis for the engendering of the intelligible world. She highlights the "unacknowledged and unrepayable debt that the very notion of space, and the built environment that relies on its formulation, owe to what Plato characterizes as the 'femininity' of the chora".[12] Grosz also aligns her argument with Irigaray's reading of the history of philosophy as the erasure of women's autonomy and worth:

Irigaray claims that masculine modes of thought have performed a devastating sleight of hand: they have obliterated the debt they owe to the most primordial of all spaces, the maternal space from which all subjects emerge, and which they ceaselessly attempt to usurp [...] The production of a [male] world – the construction of an 'artificial' or cultural environment, the production of an intelligible universe, religion, philosophy, the creation of true knowledge and valid practices of and in that universe – is implicated in the systematic and violent erasure of the contributions of women, femininity and the maternal. This erasure is the foundation or ground on which thoroughly masculine world is built.[13]

However, the absence of Ottoman imperial women in visual material was not exactly a simple act of subordination. It was not even, as Coleman suggests, "the total eclipsing of the feminine."[14] The so-called period of the 'Sultanate of Women' (sometimes referred to as the 'Reign of Women')—which began in 1520, during Süleyman the

Magnificent's rule, and continued until 1656, ending with Turhan Hatice Sultan as *valide sultan* and her son, Mehmed IV, as sultan—can be seen as a period where women played a 'masculine' game.[15] Despite doing so from a restricted space, the financial power at their disposal gave them the freedom to undertake expensive building projects, and therefore, demonstrate their presence in society. While, from a post-modern female perspective, it may seem that they were merely objects of male sexual gratification, this was clearly not the case. In fact, the Imperial *Harem* was a sacred and private space for women, and the sultanate became the ground from which they set out to assert their power and authority.[16]

The Space of 'Otherness and the Ottoman Imperial Harem

For the purpose of this study, a contemporary architectural perspective that uses the theory of 'otherness', which is associated with everyday spaces (e.g., the *harem*), is of primary interest. By using such a perspective two groups of scholars emerge, and both seek to "find an architectural equivalent or parallel to the writings of Jacques Derrida's [...] notion of difference".[17] Derrida's critical outlook concerned with the relationship between text and meaning in this scenario mirrors the relationship between women of the *harem* and the meanings associated with their building projects. The first group, de-constructivists like Peter Eisenman, challenge Derrida's notion, with respect to architecture. Eisenman claims that, "binary oppositions such as form and content or structure and decoration are inscribed within a seemingly fixed, hierarchical structure and then eroded by the second or subordinate term in the opposition, [therefore,] the value system of architecture itself is eroded and put into flux".[18] If viewed from Eisenman's perspective, the *harem* quarters of the imperial Ottoman women represent a hierarchical structure that was established within the compound, architecturally, as well as in terms of private spaces that were allocated to specific individuals, i.e., women, such as the *valide sultan*—with the sultan's quarters on one side and those of the eunuchs on the other. However, whether this represented an 'erosion of', 'subordination to' or nothing more than a 'separation from' the public space (*selamlik*), which was mostly occupied by the males of Topkapı

Palace, the powerful influence of *harem* women over the sultan cannot be denied. Additionally, the fact that the *harem* walls adjoined those of the Divan Council chambers, may, as Eisenman suggests, primarily be about 'presence'. Therefore, the notion of 'otherness' is secondary because "the presence of absence [... of this] other architecture [...] this second text will always be within the first text [...] and thus between traditional presence and absence, between being and non-being".[19] The women's "presence of absence", as espoused by Eisenman, can be seen in the mosque complexes of the women, which adorn the skyline of Istanbul today. Like the sultanic imperial mosques of Mehmed II and Süleyman the Magnificent, the imperial mosques of Hürrem Sultan, Mihrimah Sultan and Nurbanu Sultan, after four and a half centuries, continue to reinforce their "presence", but not their "absence", as *equal* players in the creation of the visual narrative of sixteenth-century Ottoman Istanbul. the geographic division between the gendered mosques: one on Eur side of Bosphorus, one on Turkish side – anything more on that?

The second group of scholars, which included Edward Soja[20] and Anthony Vidler[21] looks to Michel Foucault's notion of "heterotopia", based on his 1967 essay "Des Espaces autre" (*Of Other Spaces: Utopias and Heterotopias*), which discusses physical spaces. In his essay, Foucault distinguishes heterotopias between imaginary spaces and everyday landscapes, which he describes as spaces that have more layers of meaning and more connections to other places than may initially be realised. According to Foucault, heterotopia is a physical representation of an utopia, and by using the mirror as a metaphor for duality and contradictions—where on the one hand the image in the mirror is not real, but on the other hand the mirror itself is a real object —he discusses how the way in which one relates to his/her own image is shaped. Within this framework, Foucault describes 'other' places, for example, museums, theatres, prisons, churches, hospitals and brothels. To this list, we could also add *harem* as a place of 'imagined' utopia, and specifically with regard to the Imperial Harem, a place where the orientalist male's sexual fantasies and female power and sovereignty, co-exist. Furthermore, Foucault suggests that such heterotopic environments are both privileged and politically charged places:

> Heterotopias always presuppose a system of opening and closing that both isolates them and makes them penetrable. In general, the heterotopic site is not freely accessible like a public place.[22]

Considering the *harem* as a space of 'otherness', which is both 'isolated' from the public, yet also 'penetrable', reinforces the contradiction that the private *haremlik* space came to play in the lives of Ottoman imperial women. Between Derrida's *difference* where actions at a number of heterogeneous features that govern the production of meaning,[23] and Foucault's notion of 'otherness', Ottoman royal women and the spaces they occupied—both in private, as seen in the *harem* compound, and their very public imperial mosque complexes—came to display a political and social vision of Ottoman architecture that exclusively focuses on the 'other' as different, and is, therefore, politically positioned. Given this perspective, how did women successfully subvert societal norms and challenging patriarchal power relations during the Süleymanic period?

Legitimising Ottoman Imperial Women's Sovereignty

Orientalist representations of the Ottoman *harem* have contributed to much of the West's misconceptions about the role of royal women in Ottoman society. According to Ebru Boyar and Kate Fleet,

> [...] the view of Ottoman woman as relegated to the roles of wives and mothers, at least before the nineteenth century, still persists and little scholarly attention has been paid to women as active participant in the public space, visible, present and an essential element in the everyday, public life of the empire.[24]

For example, a sixteenth century traveller to Istanbul, Hans Derschwam, commented that women were entirely invisible and separate from mainstream society.[25] Aslı Sancar, in *Ottoman Women: Myth and Reality*, also reinforces such misconceptions—she writes, "Ottoman women were portrayed as pitiable victims, creatures captive in the harem without any individual agency."[26] Derschwam, however, was correct in saying that women were not often seen in the public Istanbul, and in the rare cases that they were, were expected to maintain a level of 'seclusion', which was part of keeping with Islamic values and virtues, i.e., so she could maintain her reputation as a respectable member of Muslim society. This practice was not unusual and was certainly adhered to by Hürrem, Mihrimah, Nurbanu, Safiye, Kösem Mahpeyker and Turhan Hatice.[27] However, under the *kanunname* (laws) of Sultan Süleyman, devoted women were given the title *muaddere* and allowed to appear in public, but only with an escorted retinue.[28] In fact, Lucienne Thys-Senocak has shown that women were capable of achieving greater social status and mobility through their piety. Thus, their seclusion was a positive affirmation of their feminine prowess, and for women of the Imperial *Harem*, their commissions of public projects was one of the ways in which they displayed their influence without relying on their physical appearance.[29]

However, for Westerners to associate the word "harem" with others such as "veil" and "polygamy" suggests a physical oppression and seclusion of women.[30] While the *harem* did, to a degree, seclude women from society, it was also an institution that provided women with opportunities to gain power and influence during the sixteenth and seventeenth centuries. The *harem* itself was precisely organised and structured according to a hierarchy of women, much like the *devshirme* system was organised for boys and men. The lowest class within the *harem* were servants (*cariyeler*) and the highest class belonged to the *gedikiler* (privileged ones). This structure was further broken down into sub-groups, according to the skills of each woman, and as their skills increased, the system allowed women to climb the *harem's* social ladder.[31] Therefore, despite all the misrepresentations that exist about the *harem*, one common belief held by outsiders is accurate; the *harem* was like its own little world. Additionally, the manner in which women managed affairs was unique to the *harem* and men who were not related to the women were strictly forbidden to access it.³² The *devshirme* boys were equally secluded from the women in their own *selamlik*, which was an area prescribed to men.³³ At Topkapı Palace, both women from men, and men from women, were separated from one another through its gendered architectural design. This seclusion led to the development of a private society where women established their own community and operated within their own area.³⁴ However, the boundaries within Islamic society and the boundaries imagined by many Westerners are quite different. In *Beyond Harem Walls*, Leslie Peirce has shown that the degree of social mobility was not nearly as influenced by the dichotomies of public / private or male/female, as the dichotomy of privileged / common that was seen in Europe at the time.³⁵ However, Ottoman royal women, through financial means, were able to wield influence and power all from within the confines of what would likely be termed as 'gender discrimination' today.

At the top of the *harem* hierarchy were the ranks of the *haseki* and the *valide sultan*. The *haseki* was the favourite concubine of the sultan, and exercised considerable power and influence, as was the case with Hürrem Sultan *(Figure 1)*.

Figure 1. This depiction of a haseki from Nicholas de Nicolay's stay in Istanbul in 1555 is most likely a true representation of an imperial woman of the court with her Turkish dress apart from her crown which suggests a European interpretation of a royal image. Photograph reproduction.

However, the most powerful and influential woman of the *harem* was not usually the sultan's *haseki*, but rather, the sultan's mother, the *valide sultan* ('royal mother' or 'queen mother').³⁶ In some cases, such as that of Safiye Sultan (d. 1619), the mother of Mehmed III (d. 1603), the *valide sultan* held extreme power and can be said to have ruled the Empire indirectly, as a regent for her son. In fact, this was often the case when a new sultan who was just coming to power was either too young to rule alone or mentally incapable of doing so. It is important to note, however, that some of the powerful *valide sultans* were first *hasekis*, as was the case with Nurbanu, Safiye and Kösem.[37] Although her power rested through her sexuality, i.e., in producing an heir, her reliance on male agency for this power was still paramount.

From the beginning of Sultan Süleyman's reign imperial women not only became more vocal about asserting their identity and political influence in affairs of the State, but also about leaving a lasting artistic impression on the Empire—everywhere from its capital of Istanbul to far flung provinces. This was not only demonstrated in their patronage of buildings, but also in the exchange of gifts between themselves and European monarchs.

The segregation of the sexes in the early Ottoman royal family contributed to the development of women's own hierarchical structure.[38] This political mimicking of their male counterparts highlights Irigaray's comments (above). Female networks were established as a result of women gaining access to information about the outside world and through power through alliances, in which both women on the inside and men (e.g., pashas and viziers) on the outside seeking to support their son/s accession to the throne. An example of this can be seen in the power play between Hürrem Sultan and her son-in-law, also Süleyman's Grand Vizier, Rustem Pasha. When the Grand Vizier, Ibrahim Pasha, supported Prince Mustafa—the son of Hürrem's nemesis from Süleyman's first *haseki*—Hürrem plotted against him and triumphed when the Ibrahim was executed in 1536. The female elders, mothers of princes, and occasionally of sultans, enjoyed their authority in the *harem*. In a monarchical dynastic polity, such as that of the Ottomans, it was important for the women of the imperial household, particularly the mother of the reigning sultan, to assume legitimate roles. This meant asserting her presence to her subjects like her imperial male counterparts.

Renaissance Women's Processions: Visual Metaphors of Sovereignty

During the Sultanate of Süleyman, one of the implicit ways he demonstrated his imperial authority was through iconic image ceremonies, which were spatially supported and elaborated by the architecture of the palace grounds. Three specific areas where women participated in public ceremonies included: the procession of the *valide sultan*, the circumcision ceremony of the prince(s) documented in the *Surname-i Hümayun*, and the welcoming of the sultan from a victorious campaign.

Processions of Nurbanu Sultan

One example of the high profile of the *valide sultan*, which relates to Friday prayers, belongs to Selim II's wife, Nurbanu Sultan. On an occasion when Selim II and those who followed did not attend a weekly prayer ritual, but instead retreated to the palace and his *harem*, it was left to the queen mother to represent the imperial family as the head of the community through her presence at the mosque. According to the French ambassador, Du Fresne-Canaye, Selim II had only attended Friday prayers twice in three months, which contrasted sharply with his father Suleyman who had never missed his weekly religious duties.[39] Similarly, in 1590, the Venetian ambassador Moro noted that Murad III had to be coerced by his Grand Vizier, Sinan Pasha, to make an appearance at the mosque and appease a restless populace. Therefore, Nurbanu Sultan, under similar circumstances, filled the void of her husband, Selim II's, absence from his public duties. By Nurbanu taking charge, and through the symbolism of the carriages that ferried her entire female entourage to the mosque, she was a visible sovereign in the eyes of her subjects. Such an example clearly reinforces Irigaray's comments (above) relating to the "mimicry" of women, which they used to challenge their subordination.[40]

The visual ceremony that accompanied the processions of the sultan to his palace, to Friday prayers, or from his triumphant return to Istanbul from military campaigns, in later centuries also came to include the *valide sultan* and her entourage at the accession of her son to the throne (Figures 2-3).

Figures 2, 3. Right, Austrian artist, anonymous. The carriage of the valide sultan, c.1570. Below, the Procession of the Valide Sultan. David Ungnad von Sonnegg, "Sachsische Landesbibliothek", Dresden, sixteenth century. Photograph reproductions.

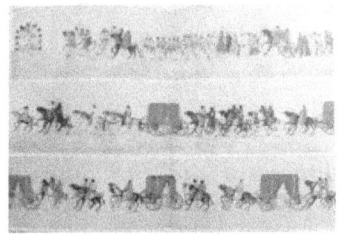

While there are only a few surviving European watercolour sketches that depict the procession of the *valide sultan* and the wedding ceremonies of princesses, which occurred in the sixteenth and sevententh centuries, they offer impressions of what such processions looked like. In fact, in the later part of the period sultanic processions came to influence the courts of Europe; where imitating Ottoman visual tastes became the fashion. The first painting by an anonymous Austrian artist in 1570 depicts the carriage of Nurbanu Sultan. It is in full sight of the public, but Nurbanu's presence teases the audience as she can only be glimpsed in the split of the velvet at the opening of the carriage, which creates suspense about her looks. The second, from David Ungnad von Sonnegg's album (c.1581/86?), shows the large and colourful entourage of her Highness, with other *harem* women attendees and black eunuchs, heading to the Topkapı Palace entrance in four royal carriages, also with their draperies half open to suggest her royal presence. Based on the date of the painting, the procession may be that of either Nurbanu Sultan or Safiye Sultan. For Peirce,

> [v]irtually all echelons of the governing elite were represented in the procession: the palace hierarchy as well as the outer administration, the military establishment as well as the religious institution. As the procession made its way across the city of Istanbul, the *valide sultan* received the obeisance of the agha of the Janissaries and in turn distributed bonuses to his troops [...] The valide sultan was received in the palace by her son, who awaited her son on foot

and greeted her with obeisance (an honor accorded by the sultan to no other person). She marked her installation in her new office and residence by dispatching to the grand vizier on the day after the procession an imperial order giving him formal notice of her arrival, which she accompanied with the gift of a ceremonial robe of honor and a dagger.[41]

Being welcomed by the Sultan at the palace gate, with a salutation not given to anybody else, demonstrates the power of the *Valide* Sultan.

From watercolour sketches to later orientalist paintings, it becomes apparent that the drapery on the carriage and the colour of the tent defines the Ottoman royal women's presence amidst her subjects, whilst also heightening their anticipation and the suspense that surrounds her physical identity (*Figures 4*).

Figure 4. Lambert de Vos, detail from an album illustration of the wedding procession of a princess, 1574. Der Staats-und Universitatsbibliothek, Bremen. Photograph reproduction.

Figure 5. 1737 painting by Jean-Baptiste Vanmour of a marriage procession provides an insight into what may have happened similarly with the Valide Sultan's own procession to the Topkapı Palace. Photograph reproduction.

It is through such visual splendour—filled with symbolism—that the status of royal women was further cemented. Furthermore, the public profile of women who became a *valide sultan* was maintained by rituals, worthy of their status, that accompanied them on every trip outside the palace—regardless of whether the destination was another residence, Friday prayers at mosque, or garden. In an unprecedented late sixteenth century painting of a woman of the *harem* (indicated by the presence of black eunuch on horseback who follows the wedding carriage) with her face on full display, is shown dressed in a tiara and regal attire, which further reinforces Sonnegg's portrayal in Figure 3 (above) of the *Valide's* grandiose ceremonial arrival at the palace (*Figure 6*).

Figure 6. A wedding procession of women of the harem. Landesbibliothek und Murkardsche Bibliothek, c.1580. Photograph reproduction.

Not only the women's physical presence was made possible through their procession but, as Boyar and Fleet writes, "the olfactory space be taken into account" when considering their presence in society. Evliya Çelebi, the 17th century Ottoman traveller writes of his experience passing a wedding procession: "[...] even from a distance of ten paces my brain was suffused with fragrances."[42] The symbolism of the procession ceremonies depicted above, suggests the public did not only endorse the role of the *Valide* Sultan, but that she was also the head of her son's private household; as a partner in Sultanic sovereignty.

Ceremonial Processions of Elizabeth I

The pen and ink drawings of the coronation procession of Elizabeth I in 1558 shows the lay-out of the dais-end of Westminster Hall for the banquet and the arrangement of the central space around the throne and up to St Edward's Chapel in the Abbey. Here, one sees a similar hierarchical visual representation of the pageantry that followed the soon to be crowned Queen (*Figure 7*).

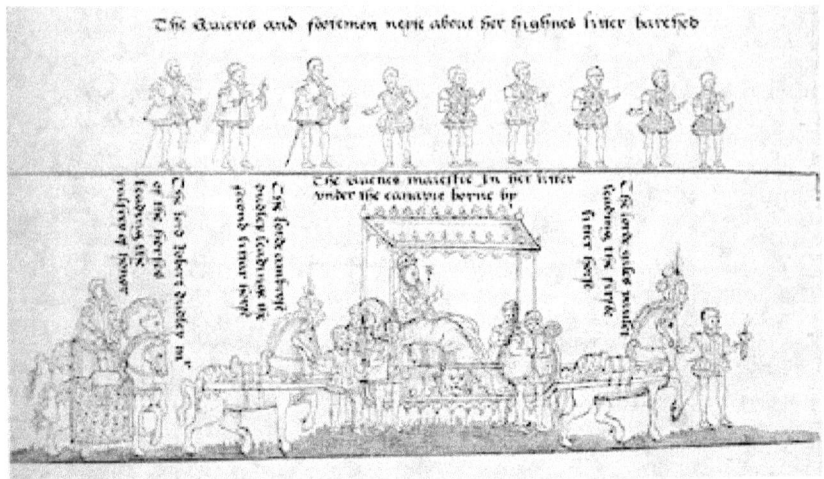

Figure 7. Ink drawing of Coronation of Elizabeth I 1558. Photograph reproduction.

This official sketch of the procession approved by the Queen herself signifies her assertion of her authority and exercising her legitimacy where, she, like the Ottoman royal women faced criticism from the intellectuals of the period laying blame on them for the woes of the state. Echoing Mustafa Ali and Celalzade Mustafa Çelebi's criticisms of the Valide Sultans, the English historian of the period William Camden similarly states: "Certainly the state of England lay now most afflicted, embroiled on the one side with the Scottish, on the other side with the French war, overcharged with debt ... the treasure exhausted; Calais ... lost, to the great dishonour of the English nation; the people distracted with different opinions in religion; the Queen bare of potent friends, and strengthened with no alliance of foreign princes."[43] The suggestion that the English sovereign is a woman may have left her without allies to defend England. Thus, the processions of these women as sovereigns of the state became visual representations of assertions of power in the face of patriarchal opposition. These pageants, therefore, came to both reject and oppose that it was the fault of "the woman who had landed the country in such a mess."[44]

Although the Ottoman royal women were not crowned as 'queens' like their Renaissance counterparts, their ceremonial processions demonstrated the pomp and splendour of their European rivals. As seen with the Valide Sultan's procession ceremonies in sixteenth century Ottoman Istanbul where all echelons of the governing elite preceded her arrival to the Topkapı Palace, a similar staging can be seen in the coronation ceremony of Elizabeth I. Before the arrival of the Queen at the Abbey, historian Rowse states:

> We see the head of it there entering the gate of Whitehall Palace, while the first folio shows us the procession being wound up by the Queen's guard just emerging from a gateway of the Tower of London. The procession follows a logical order of precedence, beginning with the messengers of the Queen's privy chamber, with the serjeant-porter, who was responsible for the entrance-gate to the royal residences, and the gentleman-harbinger, whose duty it was to make the residence ready on the approach of the Queen. Then come her personal servants, gentleman-ushers and sewers of the chamber, followed by the squires of the body and the aldermen of London. Next are the chaplains and clerks, clerks of the privy council, of the privy seal and the signet. Now the masters in chancery, the law-serjeants and the judges, with the Lord Chief Baron and the Lord Chief Justice of Common Pleas, the Master of the Rolls and the Lord Chief Justice of England walking two by two. Next come the knights and the peers, spiritual and temporal, in their proper order.[45]

Such theatrical display and the building of excitement with the arrival of the Queen at the Abbey for the commencement of her coronation ceremony resembles the greeting of the Valide Sultan at the Gate of Felicity at the Topkapı Palace by her Sultan son, the pashas, viziers and harem women signifying her status as co-ruler of the empire. While her Ottoman counterpart, the Valide Sultan, after her ceremonial procession and arrival at the seat of power presented the Grand Vizier, the robe of honour and a dagger as symbols her royal power and authority, equally, after her anointment and the commencement of the mass by Bishop of Carlisle, Elizabeth was presented with symbols of power: the royal sword, sceptre and orb signifying her role as Defender of the Faith and as Supreme Governor of the Church of England. Such powerful symbolisms clearly demonstrate the similar framework through which gender power relations were employed during the Renaissance whereby women asserted their sovereignty.

Legitimising Female Sovereignty: Funeral Processions of Nurbanu Sultan and Elizabeth I

Likewise, in death too, these Renaissance women on both sides of the cultural divide through their funeral processions demonstrate not only the respect bestowed on them by their respective subjects but the continued power they came to exude. In death, too, the reverence for Nurbanu Sultan's former status was not forgotten, and by the latter part of the sixteenth century the symbolism attached to the funeral processions of *valide sultans* represented the power and respect that were awarded to mothers of sultans. In fact, it may be that, given the respect shown by the ruling elite and the janissaries at the funeral of Nurbanu Sultan, depicted in Lokman's miniature, the *hasekis* and other women of the *harem*, seen on the left of the image, would have been given similar ceremonies *(Figure 8)*. From the court historian Selaniki's description of the stately funeral procession of the Valide Sultan one gains an impression of the respect bestowed on this Ottoman-Venetian 'Queen' Nurbanu:

> On Wednesday, 7 December 1581, the mother of his highness the caliphate-protecting sultan [...] who was a patroness of pious foundations, passed away from this transitory world to the palace of eternity by the will of God in her garden palace at the Yenikapi quarter. All the great ulema, the honourable shaykhs, and the pillars of the state walked alongside her coffin, while his highness [...] followed on foot behind them with tearful eyes, wearing a

robe of mourning up to the mosque of Sultan Mehmed II [...] where the common people had gathered [...]⁴⁶

Figure 8. A miniature painting by Lokman depicting the funeral procession of Nurbanu Sultan, c.1581. Photograph reproduction.

At the conclusion of the funeral prayers at the Conqueror's mosque, symbolising her royal status with the greatness of Ottoman lineage, Selaniki informs of her burial in the mausoleum of Selim II at Aya Sofya where for forty days the grand viziers and chief judges did not fail in their attendance day and night to pray for her soul. "The Koran was recited from beginning to end, litanies in praise of God were sung, and large sums of money and food were distributed as alms to the poor and the needy."⁴⁷

Similarly, on 28th April 1603, the death of Queen Elizabeth I was marked by a great funeral procession from Whitehall to Westminster Abbey. Two drawings of the funeral procession of Elizabeth I exist, providing an interesting account of the event. Eighteenth century reproduction of the pen and ink drawing attributed to William Camden (1551-1623) housed at the University College Oxford depict the mourners, commoners, noblemen, men, women, and children who walked ahead of Elizabeth I's effigy. The drawings also depict knight marshals clearing the way. At the end of the procession, Elizabeth's effigy is carried beneath a canopy on a chariot drawn by four horses and flanked by six barons carrying *banderoles*⁴⁸ (*Figure 9*).

Figure 9. William Camden's (1551-1623) funeral procession of Elizabeth I. Photograph reproduction.

Surname-i Hümayun: Ottoman 'Queens' on a Renaissance Stage – Front and Centre

Like her Elizabethan counterpart, the leading woman of the *harem*, the *valide* exercised considerable power. For example, she held power over other women who would ultimately succeed her as head of the *harem*, and in order to create political ties with the outside world she arranged the marriages of princesses to pashas and viziers, which increased her influence over the governing offices under the sultan. Additionally, she was highly sought after by foreign diplomats for the purposes of acquiring trade concessions from the sultan, due to her influence over her son. While these examples do not represent an exhaustive list, they are a testament to the achievements of Ottoman royal women in spite of the gender inequalities and seclusion of females during the period.[49]

By Murad III's reign (1574-1595) and the growing power of women in the Imperial *Harem*, the order of Ottoman social dynamics had begun to change. Through an alternative reading of the *Surname-i Hümayun* manuscript, the representations of women, both imperial and 'common', may on the surface appear to remain within the societal and religious boundaries of the time. However, as Terzioğlu explains,

"Ottoman miniatures and contemporary descriptions of imperial ceremony such as the Circumcision Festival of Murad III in 1582, with its many stagelike props, reveal a fascination with the skilful manipulation of boundaries separating the viewer and the viewed, the producers and consumers of spectacle."[50] With the background setting of the ancient Roman / Byzantine Hippodrome the Renaissance stage is set for the Ottoman imperial women to make their royal appearance at the circumcision festival.

After closer analysis, the manuscript appears to illuminate and subvert traditionalist views about the absence of royal women from Ottoman society. In relation to imperial women, while their physical presence is acknowledged through the architecture of the pavilions, had the pavilions also been decorated like mosques with floral motifs painted on them, they would not have appeared out of place. In fact, by adhering to the social conventions of the period, the presence of the pavilions erected next to the Sultan's balcony would have provided much joy and respect for the royal family, particularly considering the popularity of *Valide* Nurbanu Sultan. According to D. Fairchild Ruggles, such "space-occupying objects, are not only literally present themselves but also denote a representational 'presence'."[51] While such representations of Ottoman royal women resonate with Micklewright's analysis of female images by male artists, for male viewing. [52] The strict conventions of Ottoman Islam appear to have been broken or subverted in the *Surname-i Hümayun* manuscript because the imperial women are depicted among, and in front of, the men. In other words, these women are represented as possessing an equal playing status in the functioning of everyday life, and therefore, the idea of *haremlik / selamlik* or private / public space between genders becomes blurred.

The growing power of Ottoman royal women is also exemplified in the architectural layout of the viewing spaces, which the *Surname-i Hümayun* shows as having been allocated to royal parties. While the Sultan and his son occupy the balcony of the audience hall of the palace, situated to the right of the Valide Sultan's pavilion, they are also shown to have been accompanied by his sword-bearer and ewer-bearer, both of whom can be seen across all folios, standing behind the

Sultan and the Prince. In the Sultan's space another small balcony is noticeable, to the left, facing his mother's pavilion. This architectural symbolism, once again, signifies the close relationship that existed between Murad III and his mother, Nurbanu Sultan, and reinforces the female sovereignty of the Empire.

However, while the *Surname-i Hümayun* mentions that the women of the Sultan's household were taken to Ibrahim Pasha's palace, there is no further mention of them. The only visibility of their presence is through the depictions of the pavilions with lattice windows. According to Boyar and Fleet,

> Although concealed, they [women] could be heard through the lattice work of the *cumba* (bay window), through which they themselves could see the street below, or while watching a *Karagöz* play from behind a screen [...][53]

The lattice window not only served to accentuate the presence of imperial women in public spaces, it also served an artistic purpose. The significance of the lattice window in Ottoman art was just as important as perspective was to Renaissance painting, and Hans Belting explains its importance in his analysis of the geometry of the *muqarnas*:

> Plane perspective, in which three dimensions are projected to make a two-dimensional, follows the principle of spatial vision and requires us to ignore the surface and "see through" it. In Islamic culture the surface is preserved; it even acquires greater value as the site of computation and perception, becoming [...] almost sacred. When it takes the form of a lattice window (*mashrabiyya*), a surface pattern made of light, it is reflected on the floor walls of a room.[54]

In other words, ignoring the surface and allowing the viewer to imagine the interior reinforce the image of 'woman as sacred'. Just as the mosques of the imperial women, their 'sacred' status in Ottoman dynasty kept in line with the Islamic model of the Prophet's wives as "mothers of believers", and from art forms such as miniatures to architectural monuments, the royal ladies are represented as such.

When it came to the women of the *harem*, organisers built a raised pavilion with red wooden grillwork facing the first courtyard of the palace, which was most likely reserved for the Sultan's mother, Nurbanu Sultan, and the mother of the Prince, Safiye Sultan, as well as their ladies and eunuchs *(Figure 10)*.

Figure 10. Folios 42b (left), 43a (right). Horsemen parading before the Sultan and the women of the Imperial Harem of the Valide Sultan; the juxtaposition of the distance of Sultan and his son from his subjects seen in the balcony to the top left of the miniature painting in folio 42b, to the closeness of the Valide Sultan's pavilion to the foreign dignitaries and her subjects symbolising her power can easily be seen in folio 43a. 1582 Surname-i Hümayun by Lokman. Photograph reproduction.

According to Atasoy and Bragner, the Valide Sultan's (Queen Mother) entourage arrived in 53 carriages.[55] Another pavilion with lattice windows, to the left of the ladies' apartment, would likely have also been allocated to the Valide Sultan, and perhaps the mother of the Prince, for private viewing of the festivities outside the palace. In the early folios, 14b-15a and 18b-19a, this structure appears as a single level. However, in later folios, 32b-33a, second level has been added and remains as such until the end of the manuscript, which indicates that a greater number of imperial household members attended the festivities of later years.

The use of the screen, as part of the gendered architecture by the architects of the pavilions, removes the Hippodrome and the world from the gaze of the women who view from within. The figures on the outside become geometric patterns, from the public's perspective; these make a stronger impression than the blurry forms behind it. In essence, the architects laid a veil between the Valide Sultan and her subjects, and therefore, what she saw was mediated by her cultural heritage.[56] As with imperial women's architecture, their presence in the above scenario is once again represented by the manipulation of light, which draws the gaze of those inhabiting the space inside the pavilion to look outside. Therefore, in this context, just as in Renaissance Italy, light was used as a cultural symbol. However, in Islamic art (as opposed to Renaissance paintings) light is not produced in the human gaze but created through decoration that filters and regulates it. Thus, the lattice windows and their geometry serve as a stage for a symbolic form of light, that is, where outside and inside worlds relate differently to one another, and different roles are assigned to the observer and the observed.[57] However, to go as far as claiming that the role of the subject is inactive, Belting has suggested, would be misleading and erroneous within the Ottoman context.[58] After all, the positioning of the Valide Sultan's pavilion, in relation to the Sultan's balcony distanced from his subjects and the stand of the foreign dignitaries, clearly negates such a perspective. Instead, the central presence of the imperial women with their close proximity to the celebrations and the people only promotes their power and sovereignty for their subjects.

According to Thys-Senocak, one of the most interesting features of gendered architecture is the manipulation of gaze.[59] Within the

Surname-i Hümayun, the centrality of the pavilions, particularly that of the Valide Sultan demonstrates her significant role as a political mediator, and by manipulating gaze, the architects of these structures ensured that she and her ladies had viewing access to all the festivities. Additionally, the arrival of her entourage and her place in the pavilion ensure that the Valide Sultan and her pavilion are the centre-piece of the public's gaze. This further reaffirms her elevated status, that is, through the "inaccessibility, and inviolable space that separated the members of the imperial procession from their Ottoman subjects."[60] Further in the manuscript, through its depiction of the entourage settled within the pavilion, the object that, moments earlier, had been the focus of the public's gaze suddenly represents a position of privilege and authority; seating those who can control the gaze (and lives) of their subjects.[61]

Another point of significance in the *Surname-i Hümayun* is that the Valide Sultan's viewing pavilion is situated between the Sultan's balcony and the official dignitaries' stand, as symbolic reference to the sovereignty exercised by the 'Sultanate of Women' during the period. It also represents how women could hold power that was equal to that of men; in negotiations and government affairs and through the formation of alliances with pashas and viziers (on the outside of the *harem*), which would strengthen their position inside the *harem*.

Conclusively, representations of women by women and women by men have demonstrated different approaches to the concept of gender, and female authority in early modern Ottoman history. The misconceptions of the notion of the physical absence of women imposed on them by Islam remain historically inaccurate. In Ottoman architectural and visual representations, the royal women of the Ottoman Imperial *Harem* have demonstrated themselves to be active participants in the everyday life of early modern Ottoman society. Unlike the sultan, the women remained visually present, front and centre, viewing public celebrations behind lattice windows, ensuring the power of their presence signified and augmented their sovereignty to their subjects. While their power and authority remained intact, as long as their son remained on the throne, more significantly, however, they also wielded their sovereignty to their subjects by their *presence of absence* via their ostentatious royal processions and entourage. Such visual spectacle mimicking the sultan's own processions allowed the imperial women to subvert the Ottoman patriarchal order and assert their own sovereignty as co-rulers of the empire with their sons. Lastly, like the coronation and funeral processions of Elizabeth I, the Ottoman imperial women, similarly demonstrated their authority as female sovereigns of an empire wielding such power over their male counterparts.

Bibliography

Ahmed, Leila. "Western Ethnocentrism and Perceptions of the Harem." *Feminist Studies* 8, 3 (1982): 522-523. Accessed February 23, 2015. http://www.jstor.org/.

Aksit, Ilhan. *The Mystery of the Ottoman Harem.* Istanbul: Aksit Kültür Ve Turizm Yayıncıl, 2005.

Atasoy, Nurhan and Robert Bragner. *1582 Surname-i Hümayun: An Imperial Celebration.* Istanbul: Koçbank, 1997.

Belting, Hans. *Florence and Baghdad: Renaissance Art and Arab Science.* Translated by Deborah Lucas Schneider. Cambridge: The Belknap Press of Harvard University Press, 2011.

Boyar, Ebru and Kate Fleet, eds. *Ottoman Women in Public Space.* Leiden: Brill, 2016.

Camden, William. *History of the Most Renowned and Victorious Princess Elizabeth.* London: E. Flesher for Charles Harper and John Amery, 1675.

Coleman, Debra. "Introduction." In *Architecture and Feminism.* Edited by Debra Coleman, Elizabeth Denza, and Carol Henderson, ix-xvi. New York: Princeton Architectural Press, 1996.

Çelebi, Evliya. *Seyahatname*, IV. Edited by Yücel Dağli and Seyit Ali Kahraman. Istanbul: Yapı Kredi Yayınları, 2001.

Embassy to Constantinople: The Travels of Lady Mary Wortley Montagu. Edited by Christopher Pick, with an introduction by Dervla Murphy. London: Century, 1988.

Ergin, Nina. "Ottoman royal women's spaces: the acoustic dimension," *Journal of Women's History* 26, 1 (2014): 89-111.

Ferguson, M. W., M. Quilligan and N. J. Vickers, eds. *Rewriting the Renaissance: The Discourses of Sexual Difference in Early Modern Europe*. Chicago: University of Chicago Press, 1986.

Freely, John. *Inside the Seraglio: Private Lives of the Sultans in Istanbul*. London: Penguin Books Ltd., 1999.

Fresne-Canaye, Philippe Du. *Le Voyage du Levant de Philippe du Fresne-Canaye, 1573*. Translated by M. H. Houser. London: British Library, 2011.

Goodwin, Godfrey. *A History of Ottoman Architecture*. London, UK: Thames and Hudson, 1971.

Grosz, Elizabeth. "Women, *Chora*, Dwelling." In *Postmodern Cities and Spaces*, edited by Sophie Watson and Katherine Gibson, 35-50. Oxford: Blackwell Publishers, 1995.

Gülen, Salih. *The Ottoman Sultans: Mighty Guests of the Throne*. Translated by Emrah Sahin. New York: Blue Dome Press, 2010.

Irigaray, Luce. *The Sex Which Is Not*. Translated by Catherine Porter and Caroline Burke. Ithaca, New York: Cornell University Press, 1985.

Kuban, Doğan. *Ottoman Architecture*. Suffolk: Antique Collectors Club Distributors, 2010.

McLeod, Mary. "Everyday and 'Other' Spaces." In *Architecture and Feminism*, edited by Debra Coleman, Elizabeth Denza, and Carol Henderson, 1-37. New York: Princeton Architectural Press, 1996.

Millingen, Fredrick. "The Circassian Slaves and the Sultan's Harem." *Journal of the Anthropological Society of London* 8 (1870-1871): cix-cxx. Accessed September 23, 2015, http://www.jstor.org/.

Mustafa Efendi, Selaniki. *Tarih-i Selaniki*. Michigan: University of Michigan Library, 1989.

Necipoğlu, Gülru. *The Age of Sinan: Architectural Culture in the Ottoman Empire*. London: Reaktion Books, 2005.

Peirce, Leslie. "Beyond Harem Walls: Ottoman Royal Women and the Exercise of Power." In *Gendered Domains: Rethinking Public and Private in Women's History*, edited by Dorothy O. Helly and Susan M. Reverby, 40-55. New York: Cornell University Press, 1992.

Peirce, Leslie. "Domesticating Sexuality: Harem Culture in Ottoman Imperial Law." In *Harem Histories: Envisioning Places and Living Spaces*, edited by Marilyn Booth, 104-135. London: Duke University Press, 2010.

Peirce. Leslie P. *The Imperial Harem: Women and Sovereignty in the Ottoman Empire*. New York: Oxford University Press, 1993.

Pohl, Nicole. *Women, Space, Utopia, 1600-1800*. Burlington: Ashgate Publishing Company, 2006.

Rowse, A. L. "The Coronation of Queen Elizabeth." *History Today* 3 (1953). Accessed September 14, 2015. http://www.historytoday.-com/al-rowse/coronation-queen-elizabeth#sthash.k2V6Uhff.dpuf

Rowse, A. L. *The England of Elizabeth*. London: Palgrave, 2003.

Ruggles, Fairchild, D. "Vision and Power: An Introduction." In *Women, Patronage and Self-Representation in Islamic Societies*, edited by D. Fairchild Ruggles, 1-16. New York: State University of New York Press, 2000.

Sancar, Aslı. *Ottoman Women: Myth and Reality*. New Jersey: The light, Inc., 2007.

Schick, Irvin Cemil. "The Harem as Gendered Space and the Spatial Reproduction of Gender." In *Harem Histories: Envisioning Places and Living Spaces*, edited by Marilyn Booth, 69-86. London: Duke University Press, 2010.

Seng, Yvonne J. "Invisible Women: Residents of Early Sixteenth-Century Istanbul." In *Women in the Medieval Islamic World: Power, Patronage, and Piety*, edited by Gavin R. G. Hambly, 241-268. New York: St. Martin's Press, 1998.

Somerset, Anne. *Elizabeth I*. London: Phoenix Giant, 1998.

Terzioğlu, Derin. "The Imperial Circumcision Festival of 1582: An Interpretation." *Muqarnas* 12 (1995): 84-100.

Thys-Senocak, Lucienne. "The Yeni Valide Mosque Complex of Eminönü Istanbul (1597-1665): Gender and Vision in Ottoman Architecture." In *Women, Patronage and Self-Representation in Islamic Societies*, edited by D. Fairchild Ruggles, 69-90. Albany: State University of New York Press, 2000.

Thys-Senocak, Lucienne. *Ottoman Women Builder: The Architectural Patronage of Hadice Turhan Sultan*. Vermont: Ashgate, 2006.

Woodward, J. *The Theatre of Death: The ritual management of royal funerals in Renaissance England, 1570-1625*. Woodbridge: Boydell Press, 1997.

Yerasimos, Stephane. "The Imperial Procession: Recreating a World's Order." In *Surname-i Vehbi*. Accessed July 3, 2015. http://web.archive.org/web/20091025054327/http://geocities.com/surnamei_vehbi/yerasimos.html

Two Queens, Three Letters and Three Gifts - Metaphors of the visual language of female sovereignty in the Early Modern Period

ESSAY III

Abstract: By integrating gender as articulated by Ottoman women sovereigns through their patronage this essay aims to challenge the misconceptions of the sultan's private space, the Imperial *Harem*, as merely a place of sexual orgies as perpetuated by orientalist discourse. Contrary to this erroneous assertion, this article demonstrates the political assertiveness of Ottoman imperial women as sovereigns in their own right. This assertion of female agency is evident in the Ottoman imperial woman – Safiye Sultan (d. 1619), the *haseki* (favourite) of Murad III and after his death in 1595, as the Valide Sultan (Queen Mother) of Mehmed III (d. 1603). Through her exchange of letters and gifts as visual medium with Elizabeth I of England, Safiye Sultan, thus, challenges the illusion of seclusion of Ottoman imperial women through the metaphors of visual language of these gifts to assert her sovereignty.

Keywords: *sovereignty, legitimacy, queen, haseki, valide sultan, imperial harem*

> By investigating how women of the Ottoman court wrote to individuals of different social ranking ... it will become possible to gain a deeper understanding of the balance of power in a wide range of relationships these women maintained.[1]

Bernadette Andrea in *Women and Islam in Early Modern English Literature* explores the political assertiveness of women in the early modern period. She proposes that women of the sixteenth century "as objectified female speaking itself constituted a radical assertion of agency."[2] Andrea has focused on the letters between the two queens "to assess Elizabeth's paradoxical position as a 'female prince' and "the parallel patriarchal dismissal of women's sovereignty in the Ottoman Empire and the West."[3] With these two women the author is showing through the use of the literary medium the shared signifiers of femininity to establish their sovereignty in their respective patriarchal cultures.[4] This article, therefore, explores the symbolisms of the correspondence and exchange of gifts between Safiye Sultan and Elizabeth I where the illusion of seclusion changes to a representation of reality, that is, of the sovereignty of Ottoman royal women by subverting patriarchal norms. It takes Bernadette Andrea's framework further by addressing the exchange of gifts between these two women beyond the literary discourse and through the use of the gifts as visual medium "[...] negotiating the paradoxical position of the sovereign women within their respective patriarchal cultures" where "they become 'objects that speak' as agents of cross-cultural exchange."[5] This demonstrates the fluidity of Renaissance cultures in the early modern period where the Ottomans, including the imperial women of the *harem*, were active participants.

Feminist Methodology

Mirroring the males by females in sixteenth century Ottoman imperial *harem*, highlight the significance of women asserting their sovereignty in the patriarchal world. The French feminist philosopher, Luce Irigaray, states that in order for women from history to assign to the feminine they had to resort to "mimicry", and convert "a form of subordination into an affirmation, and thus to begin to thwart it."[6] According to Irigaray, women demand to speak as a masculine "subject", and through mimesis, a woman attempts to recover her place from exploitation by discourse: "without allowing herself to be simply reduced to it. It means to resubmit herself – inasmuch as she is on the side of the "perceptible" of "matter" – to "ideas" in particular to ideas about herself, that are elaborated in/by a masculine logic."[7] By applying this *universal* interpretation to Ottoman imperial woman of the sixteenth and seventeenth centuries, it may be said that through their engagement with the outside world including the use of gifts as objects of exchange, they demonstrate their subversion of the Ottoman patriarchal social order, and negate being "products" for use and exchange by men.[8] Furthermore, through this demonstration of masculine mimesis, "even though she is hidden, most often hidden as woman and absent in the capacity of subject, manages to make 'sense' [...] manages to create 'content'."[9]

Similarly, Elizabeth Grosz also aligns her argument with Irigaray's reading of the history of philosophy as the erasure of women's autonomy and worth. Grosz states:

> Irigaray claims that masculine modes of thought have performed a devastating sleight of hand: they have obliterated the debt they owe to the most primordial of all spaces, the maternal space from which all subjects emerge, and which they ceaselessly attempt to usurp [...] The production of a [male] world – the construction of an 'artificial' or cultural environment, the production of an intelligible universe, religion, philosophy, the creation of true knowledge and valid practices of and in that universe – is implicated in the systematic and violent erasure of the contributions of women, femininity and the maternal. This erasure is the foundation or ground on which thoroughly masculine world is built.[10]

However, the absence of Ottoman imperial women in visual material was not exactly a simple act of subordination. It was not even, as Coleman suggests, "the total eclipsing of the feminine."[11] The so-called period of the 'Sultanate of Women' (sometimes referred to as the 'Reign of Women')—which began in 1520, during Süleyman the Magnificent's rule, and continued until 1656, ending with Turhan Hatice Sultan as *valide sultan* and her son, Mehmed IV, as sultan—can be seen as a period where women played a 'masculine' game.[12] Despite doing so from a restricted space, the financial power at their disposal gave them the freedom to undertake expensive building projects, and therefore, demonstrate their presence in society. While, from a post-modern female perspective, it may seem that they were merely objects of male sexual gratification, this was clearly not the case. In fact, the Imperial *Harem* was a sacred and private space for women, and the sultanate became the ground from which they set out to assert their power and authority.[13]

Safiye Sultan (1550-1619)

By 1595 Safiye Sultan, *haseki* (favourite) of Murad III, was third in line to rule as valide sultan after Hürrem (wife of Sultan Süleyman, d.1566). "Moreover, as she engaged in an extended correspondence with Queen Elizabeth I, she presents a crucial case for analysing contested representations of women's sovereignty" during the last quarter of the sixteenth century.[14] Not only did the two women exchange correspondence but they also exchanged gifts. All this must be located within Safiye Sultan's institutional role in the Ottoman power structure. The letters and exchange of gifts must also be situated within the political and economic accord between the Ottoman Empire and England. Indeed, the first of Safiye's letters became famous when the translation appeared in Richard Hakluyt's *The Principal Navigations, Voyagers, Traffiques and Discoveries of the English Nation (1590-1600)* to reinforce the growing relations between England and the Ottomans. The Turkish original of the letter is preserved in the British Museum and S. A. Skilliter published it in *Documents from Islamic Chanceries*. The second and third letters were discovered by Akdes Kurat in the Public Record Office and were published by him also appearing in Skilliter's document. As the letters were sent in both Ottoman Turkish and Italian languages there exists Italian translations of all three letters.

According to Maria Pia Pedani, the valide sultan was of Venetian background named Sofia Bellicui Baffo (1550-1605). She was taken captive by pirates in 1562 at the age of 13 and presented to the future Murad III as a slave by Huma, the granddaughter of Süleyman the Magnificent.[15] When Safiye became the Valide Sultan upon the accession of her Mehmed III in 1595 to exercise her imperial authority she not only supervised the training of the female servants of the *harem* but cultivated political alliances to assert her sovereignty as a woman. As Valide Sultan, Safiye's role was to protect the interests of her son and act as one of his top advisors. As a Muslim convert she had to demonstrate her piety to her people by maintaining the public image of the dynasty through her charitable works and the building complex of her mosque. Between 1595-1603 Safiye Sultan as a woman embodied sovereignty.

Letters from Safiye Sultan to Elizabeth I: "crowned lady and woman of Mary's way"

Relations between the Ottoman Empire and England date to Elizabeth I's initiatives to commence trade with Murad III. Between 1579 and 1581 several letters were sent to the sultan stressing the religious connections between the English Protestants and Ottoman Muslims. The anti-Catholic tone of her letters found support with the sultan when she presents herself as "the most invincible and most mighty defender of the Christian faith against all kinds of idolatries, of all that live among the Christians, and falsly protesse the Name of Christ."[16] It is, therefore, through the weight of economic concessions to the English that Safiye and Elizabeth begin their exchange of a series of letters and gifts further confirming the Ottoman-Anglo political, economic and cultural ties. This correspondence between the two women, each trying to legitimise their sovereignty in a patriarchal domain established an "unprecedented political and personal relationship."[17]

Safiye's letter of 1593 achieved prominence when Hakluyt published them. However, he incorrectly identified Safiye as the "mighty Empress the wife of the Gran Signior Sultan Murad Can."[18] Hakluyt's marginal comments about Safiye's role as a "wife" and "mother" alludes to both her crucial political power as a woman and occupying a "gendered role deemed particularly well suited for initiating a correspondence with the sovereign queen of England."[19] Before analysing the exchange of gifts as visual metaphors of female sovereignty and power it is important to understand the nature of the letters between the two women especially the first letter, in itself considered as work of art to be integrated into the visual analysis.

Ottoman-Anglo relations depended on exchange of gifts in order to gain full ambassadorial rights with the Sublime Porte. To achieve this aim the English sought the support of the Imperial *Harem* through the Valide Sultan's woman representative Esperanza Malchi, a Jewish woman known by the title Kira. She served Safiye as her business agent and in all her contacts with the outside world.

Safiye's first correspondence with Elizabeth in 1593 began in her role as the *haseki* of Murad III. This represented her role as the second most important woman of the *harem* hierarchy after her mother-in-law Nurbanu Sultan. Even in her secondary status, Safiye follows the traditionally accepted formalities in her letters through invocation to God and praising His Prophet followed by the Sultan. In her choice of words she foreshadows her role as the Valide Sultan. Impressing Elizabeth then follows this with the vastness of the Ottoman realm by listing all the territories under the sultan's rule.[20] The next section of the Safiye's letter complements the gift exchange of gifts between the two by allying herself with the Queen of England through epithets stressing "their common sovereignty and femininity".[21] Safiye praises Elizabeth as:

> The support of Christian womanhood … who follow the Messiah, nearer of the marks of pomp and majesty, trailing the skirts of glory and power, she who is obeyed by princes, cradle of chastity and continence, ruler of the realm of England, crowned lady and woman of Mary's way.[22]

The masculine address to feminine form had been the official Ottoman form of correspondence with the Queen of England. Sultan Murad III follows a similar form in his letter to Elizabeth referring to her as "most sacred Queene, and noble prince […]."[23]

Safiye's use of language in her letter to Elizabeth indicates clever manipulation of gender roles. What is significant in Safiye Sultan's address to Elizabeth is that she subverts the official Ottoman correspondence of the masculine genre by "applying terms specific to a female sovereign".[24] Her use of the word choice is important to note: "Christian womanhood", "cradle", which Skilliter mentions "Mehd-i 'ulya," being "most exalted cradle" is "an honorific title of the Valide Sultan"; and her reference to "Mary's way", mother of Jesus to reinforce that there is a woman sovereign as head of a country of which she also sees herself a part. She elevates herself to a similar status as sovereign as that of her counterpart.[25] Unlike Murad's reference to Elizabeth as a "noble prince" for Safiye the queen now is the one "who is obeyed of the princes" and "ruler of the realm of England" where men follow her orders similar to Safiye's role at the Topkapı Palace.[26] As Andrea points out "although the customary Ottoman address to queens tended to re-gender them as masculine or to de-emphasize their political power as women, Safiye does neither in her letter to Elizabeth."[27]

By acknowledging the receipt of "gifts and presents" from Elizabeth's ambassador, Safiye showcasing these in the letter establishes her sovereignty:

> [This] special letter, full of marvels, whose paper was more fragrant than pure camphor and ambergris and its ink than fines musk, notifying indescribable and immeasurable consideration and love towards (me). Her well-wisher.[28]

Safiye ends her letter with references to "Agha of the Door of chastity and modesty" and "the curtain of chastity."[29] The *haseki*, according to Skilliter, is not "diminishing her sovereignty due to her feminine subject position" rather these references need to be situated within the culturally specific definition of *haram* as a sacred place. As Peirce notes, it was so named "[...] because of there not of women but of the sultan."[30] This is in contrast to the misconceptions of the *harem* perpetuated by European travellers to the Ottoman Empire as being a place of feminine oppression at the hands of masculine fantasy.[31] At the end of her letter Safiye reasserts her authority as a sovereign Ottoman royal woman by ensuring that she will promote Elizabeth's cause:

> What was expressed in the contents of Her letter became recorded by the ear of acceptance, and injustice. It caused esteem heretofore attached to that cradle of rule and dominion to increase.[32]

In a clever fashion the Valide ensures that her status as the female sovereign is addressed and reinforced by Elizabeth maintaining correspondence with her if such an exchange is to be affected:

> If She will never cease from [sending] such ... letters which foster the increase of sincerity and love, this is to be made known.[33]

The *haseki* then continues her pledge to Elizabeth "There shall never be cessation from news about Her good health arriving and news about

Her good health becoming known ... and I shall endeavour for Her aims."[34]

Interestingly when Hakluyt published the Valide's letters his alterations to her first letter downgrade her role in the Ottoman polity.[35] As shown above, Safiye's first letter follows the standard Ottoman correspondence genre by praising God and His Prophet with her future status as valide sultan, followed by references to the extent of the empire. In contrast, however, Hakluyt reordering places the relationship between Elizabeth and Safiye last. This, as Andrea points out, "elides the sovereign position of the valide sultan and it narrowly defines her (and, by implication, Elizabeth) as a mere woman."[36] Hakluyt also modifies Safiye's reference to "Mary's way" as indicated in Skilliter's literal transcription into Latin as "Maria virgine" or "the virgin Mary."[37] Thus, his version of the letter is intending to promote a patriarchal reading between the Ottoman Valide Sultan, Mary as the virgin mother, and Elizabeth as virgin queen."[38] This mis-interpretation of Safiye Sultan's letter to Elizabeth I by Hakluyt signify the justification and the legitimising of Elizabeth I as the Protestant Queen and the true representative of Christianity. As a result the Safiye Sultan's letter, "[...] was being incorporated into the Western European, and increasingly anglocentric, imperialist project."[39] This interpretation and exchange between Safiye and Elizabeth, however, must be located during a period when the Ottoman Empire was its peak and the English were not stepping into the imperialist agenda.[40]

Her letters similarly signify the scriptoral decorative nature of Sinan's use of Qur'anic calligraphy on Iznik tiles. As calligraphic artwork the Valide Sultan's first letter having suffered the ravages of the fire of 1731 at Ashburnham House, Westminster still retains some of its artistic charm and is reminiscent of typical sixteenth century Ottoman decorative arts - single sheet of oriental paper "yellowish and inclined to break at the folds."[41] The side of the paper is generously speckled with gold similar to the many paper manuscripts and bound books found at the Topkapı Palace today. The invocation is to the right of the top centre symbolising the significance and centrality of God in our actions. Skilliter has shown that the twenty-four lines of the text occupy 28cm of the lower half of the letter:

> The lines are horizontal and, contrary to the usage observed in Imperial letters, they do not curve upwards at the end, neither are they made to reach the left edge, nor are their final letters elongated as one would see in traditional calligraphic writing.[42]

However, the script is in calligraphic *naskh* format, popularised at the Ottoman court and in "partially vocalised."[43] From the transcription plate XXXVIII it is evident of the scribe changing ink colours for different letters of the Ottoman alphabet. The scribe changes the colour of the ink three times. By changing ink colour the artist considered the purely aesthetic nature of the letter, perhaps considering the female sender and recipient. By the use of black in the last line the artist suggests an intention to stress the closing of the letter. For example,

> a-b black, b-c blue, c-d crimson, d-e black, e-f gold, f-g crimson, g-h black, h-i blue, j-k scarlet, k-j black, l-m crimson.[44]

The use of different colours, black, blue, crimson, gold, and scarlet on different letters of the Ottoman script illustrate the care taken to produce this letter by Safiye's scribe. According to Fatma Türe and Birsen T. Keşoğlu, "It is hardly imaginable that Safiye had written such a letter without resorting to the help of a professional scribe."[45] This is in sharp contrast to Sultan Süleyman's letter to Francis I in 1528 relying on black ink only to convey his message to the French King. With the exception of his highly decorative personalised *tughra* dominating the centre of the letter symbolising his masculine power, authority and dominance, Safiye's exchange with Elizabeth in this effeminate style subverts the patriarchal rules and asserts her role as the female sovereign of the Ottoman Empire with its power resting not with the

Divan (Imperial Council) but the Imperial *Harem* of the palace. The array of colours used in the letter creating the rainbow effect reflects and complements the visual expression of the patriarchal subversive nature of female sovereignty. Added to the colourful calligraphy Skilliter believes the letter was torn off "because of the valuable jewel studded seal which it bore on its verso."[46] Unfortunately the seal is lost but is described in the inventory "More one shell of gould which couered the seale of the lettere to ther Magestie upon which was sett ii smale sparkes of Dyamindes and ii small sparkes of rubies bee worth 20,000 pounds."[47] Today, the letter is owned by the British Museum and has not been on display. Unfortunately, according to the museum curator, the letter today does not demonstrate its bygone aesthetic quality as it was presented to Queen Elizabeth I in the sixteenth century.[48]

Apart from its calligraphic and aesthetic nature in the *naksh* style the writing itself is in elaborate and rhyming prose with an extravagant tone. Combining the word and art as a piece of visual expression it is interesting to note that the *haseki's* letter is a "showcase of rhetoric" where her actual correspondence only occupies less than half of the twenty-four lines.[49] The rest of the letter is devoted to its aesthetic appeal to assert a feminine visual expression.

When her son Mehmed III ascended the throne in 1595, Safiye became the Valdie Sultan. Her second and third letters are sent to Elizabeth in her role as the most powerful woman in the Ottoman Empire. In the Public Record Office of Venice it is revealed that the two undated letters arrived on 26 November 1599.[50] In comparison to the first letter, in terms of artistic and visual expressions the next two letters are "extremely primitive and crude in appearance and ... also in style."[51] The first letter, thus, in its visually appealing nature is rather unique in comparison to the latter ones. However, what is not seen in the first letter but are evident in the second and third are Valide's own seal at the bottom of the paper underneath line 15. Although there is mention in the inventory of the first letter where one shell of gold covering the seal of the letter, this, however, may not be Safiye's hallmark. It remains uncertain if Safiye would have had her *own seal* as a *haseki* in

1593 or the seal would have been someone else's, when the first letter was sent. In contrast, the seal in both the second and third letters are in black ink, "the script appearing as black on white around the central lozenge and as white on black inside it".[52] The significance of the Safiye Sultan's own hallmark highlight her prominent role in the polity of the Ottoman court and her influential position with her son.

Symbols of female sovereignty: Exchange of gifts between Safiye Sultan and Elizabeth I

The exchange of gifts between the two women expresses the subversive nature of patriarchy and assertiveness of their sovereignty. Apart from her seal at the bottom of the page what is revealed in the second letter however, is Safiye's authority as the Valide. It follows the standard invocation to a Christian sovereign followed by the growing friendship between the Valide and the Queen.

After the presentation and offering of sincere greetings and abundant salutation, rose-perfumed, which emanate from pure mutual confidence and the abundance of amity, what has to be submitted and notified is this: Your letter has arrived and reached us; whatsoever you said became known to us.[53]

The Valide then continues to promote her support for Elizabeth's proposed English trading concessions. "We do not cease from admonishing our son, His Majesty the Padishah, and from telling him; 'Do act according to the treaty!'"[54] The second half of her letter from lines 16-24 concerns the gifts exchanged between the two women:

> And you sent us a coach; it has arrived and has been delivered. It had our gracious acceptance. We, too, have sent you a robe, a girdle, a sleeve, tow gold embroidered handkerchiefs, three towels, and one crown studded with pearls and rubies.[55]

However, in these set of gifts sent to Elizabeth as recorded by Richard Wragg, a member of the English ambassador's party makes a reference of "a sute of princely attire being after the Turkish fashion would for the rareness thereoff be acceptable in England [...]."[56] For Elizabeth, a queen who was conscious of her public image female dress further reinforced the legitimacy of her sovereignty.[57] These gifts as expression of visual language respectively represent each woman's preoccupation with her legitimacy as a female sovereign. They symbolise more of a "cultural capital" rather than "economic capital."[58] By taking the assessment of these gifts further this exchange enables us to conceptualise them as the means whereby these women as sovereigns "negotiated the patriarchal contradiction of female rulers without nullifying either term of this shared cultural oxymoron."[59] The third letter repeats the previous one reiterating the exchange of gifts. It must be noted that the presents sent by Safiye Sultan in 1599 are almost identical with those sent in 1593. It is uncertain in the letter as to why the Valide would do this. Perhaps this is her way of reassuring her role as the female sovereign to another of her contemporary in England. Another reason is to emphasise the integrated role of Ottoman royal women in Muslim society just as imperial mosques of valide sultans have demonstrated.

The coach sent by Elizabeth was originally intended to be given to Murad III but at the insistence of the English ambassador it was decided that it being more expensive than the organ, that it be presented to the Valide Sultan. The decision to give the more expensive gift to Safiye Sultan signifies her importance as a political power broker in the Ottoman ruling elite. This was also Elizabeth's wish, "The coache must of necessity be givne to the old Sultana ... that hir highness had ordained [...]."[60] This demonstrates her authority as a female sovereign not only within the Imperial *Harem* but her influence over her son. The coach itself as a gift to the Valide Sultan also signify freedom of movement subverting the restrictions placed on her physical freedom from the Ottoman ruling elite. Both Safiye and her son used the coach to travel around Istanbul as indicated by ambassador Henry Lello's description where "The Sultan and she have often tymes byn abroade in the Coache."[61] However, as the coach itself no longer exists, there are contemporary sketches of imperial *harem* coaches providing historians insights into the gift that Safiye Sultan must have received from Elizabeth I (*Figure 1*). Furthermore, historians also gain understanding of the existing coaches in the Topkapı Palace that provided imperial women freedom of movement to assert their presence as sovereigns by mimicking the sultans. One can surmise that Elizabeth's coach may have been appropriated into the *harem genre* by fitting latticed windows to veil in the Queen Mother (*Figure 2*).

Figure 1. Carriage of the Valide Sultan. Franz Taeschner, Alt-Stambuler Hof- und Volksleben: Ein türkisches Miniaturenalbum aus dem 17. Jahrhundert (Hanover: Lafaire, 1925). Photograph reproduction.

Figure 2. Carriage of the women of the harem. Topkapı Palace, Istanbul, Turkey.

However, as a visual medium and its easily recognisable features would have demonstrated to the public of their Queen's presence in their midst. Thus, in this manner, the Valide Sultan is subverting patriarchal restrictions placed on her and the coach, both as a physical and visual medium is demonstrating her freedom of movements to assert her presence in society as a female sovereign.

Set against this background it is important to view these exchange of gifts between Elizabeth and Safiye as the means whereby they subvert through the symbolism of the gifts the patriarchal system where women are cast as objects and men as agents of exchange.[62] Reinforcing Irigaray's views above, what these gifts as visual mediums and letters demonstrate, are that when women are successful players in patriarchal societies they position themselves between masculinity and femininity to assert their agency despite opposition from male detractors. From Elizabeth's perspective, another gift of a portrait of herself to the Valide Sultan, where she normally would have sent such a gift in the context of marriage negotiation, highlights their preference in gift giving to a female sovereign. This, as Andrea points out, "undermines the conventions governing exchanges whereby women serve as conduits for male bonding."[63] This is demonstrated in the Valide's pleasure in the portrait so much that she asked for a second one. Andrea's argument that Safiye could not reciprocate a similar gift to Elizabeth purely on the fact that Islam prohibits human representation in Islam is unfounded especially considering her power and influence on the *harem*. If she had wanted to have a portrait of herself made she could have arranged it. Considering her influential position, she demonstrated a liking of Mr Paule Pinder, the English ambassador's secretary, who "was certainly a good-looking man" when excitement and curiosity began to mount on 12 September, Safiye went by water to view the English ship, following the Sultan in his golden caique.[64] By 21 September 1599, Dallam had managed to repair the organ and had begun to erect it in Seraglio. He quotes in his Diary:

> The same Daye, our ambassador sente Mr Paule Pinder, who was then his secretarie, with a presente to the Sultana, she being at his garthen.[65]

Safiye being in the garden of the secretary anxiously waiting for her gifts from Elizabeth demonstrates her freedom of movement among foreign male diplomats most likely with her kira as go-between.

Saifiye and Elizabeth continued to exchange gifts in the course of their negotiations, including jewellery, clothing and cosmetics. Thus, the experience of womanliness by these two women through their letters and gifts demonstrate their agency rather than being imposed on them as objects of exchange. The visual language of female sovereigns subverts and nullifies the patriarchal norms imposed on them and by creating this illusion of seclusion their buildings and objects, as art are representative of female sovereignty.

Bibliography

Andrea, Bernadette. *Women and Islam in Early Modern English Literature.* Cambridge: Cambridge University Press, 2007.

Arnold, Jane. *Queen Elizabeth's Wardrobe Unlock'd.* London: Routledge, 1988.

Bourdieu, Pierre. *Language and Symbolic Power.* Edited by John B. Thompson, translated by Gino Raymond and Matthew Adamson. Cambridge, MA: Harvard University Press, 1994.

Coleman, Debra. "Introduction." In *Architecture and Feminism,* edited by Debra Coleman, Elizabeth Denza and Carol Henderson, ix-xv. New York: Princeton Architectural Press, 1996.

Dimmock, Matthew. *New Turkes: Dramatizing Islam and the Ottomans in Early Modern England.* Aldershot, UK: Ashgate, 2005.

Grosz, Elizabeth. "Women, *Chora*, Dwelling." In *Postmodern Cities and Spaces,* edited by Sophie Watson and Katherine Gibson. Oxford: Blackwell Publishers, 1995.

Hakluyt, Richard. *The Principal Navigations, Voyagers, Traffiques and Discoveries of the English Nation*, 12 vols. New York: Anis Press, 1965.

Irigaray, Luce. *The Sex Which Is Not*. Translated by Catherine Porter and Caroline Burke. Ithaca, New York: Cornell University Press, 1985.

Lewis, Bernard. *Istanbul and the Civilization of the Ottoman Empire*. London: University of Oklahoma Press, 1963.

Luschenko, Marina. "The Correspondence of Ottoman Women during the Early Modern Period (16th – 18th Centuries): Overview on the Current State of Research, Problems, and Perspectives." In *Women's Memory: The Problem of Sources*. Edited by D. Fatma Türe and Birsen T. Keşoğlu, 56-67. Newcastle: Cambridge Scholars Publishing, 2011.

Mole, John. *The Sultan's Organ: The diary of Thomas Dallam, 1599 – London to Constantinople and adventures on the way*. London: Fortune Books, 2012.

Pedani, Maria Pia. "Safiye's Household and Venetian Diplomacy." *Turcica*, 32 (2000): 11-15.

Peirce, Leslie. "Beyond Harem Walls: Ottoman Royal Women and the Exercise of Power." In *Gendered Domains: Rethinking Public and Private in Women's History*, edited by Dorothy O. Helly and Susan M. Reverby, 28-39. New York: Cornell University Press, 1992.

Peirce, Leslie, P. *Women and Sovereignty in the Ottoman Empire*. New York: Oxford University Press, 1993.

Pohl, Nocole. *Women, Space, Utopia, 1600-1800*. Burlington: Ashgate Publishing Company, 2006.

Sanderson, John. *The Travels of John Sanderson in the Levant, 1584-1602*. Edited by Sir William Foster. London: Hakluyt Society, 1931.

Skilliter, S. A. "Three Letters from the Ottoman 'Sultana' Safiye to Queen Elizabeth I." *Documents from Islamic Chanceries*, Oriental Studies III, first series. Edited by S. M. Stern, 119-157. Oxford: Bruno Cassirer, 1965.

Suleman, F. "Islamic Art at the British Museum: Strategies and Perspectives." In *Islamic Art and the Museum - Approaches to Art and Archaeology of the Muslim World in the Twenty-First Century*. Edited by B. Junod, G. Khalil, S. Weber and G. Wolf, 276-284. London: Saqi Books, 2013.

'Siyer-i Nebi' and the Early Modern Ottoman representations of Muslim Women

ESSAY IV

Abstract: This essay proposes that the religious work of *Seyid-i Nebi* (Life of Prophet Muhammad) of 1595 illustrates an alternative interpretation where the representation of Muslim women in the miniatures subvert the traditional held view of the seclusion of females in Islamic society. Ottoman Sultan Murad III's (d.1585) patronage of the illustrated manuscript, *Siyer -i Nebi* is reflective of his interest in religious iconography to create a prophetic genealogy through its symbolism linking it to the Ottoman dynasty. The Ottoman artists cleverly portrayed the 'Mothers of the Believers' and the imperial women of the Ottoman harem without their faces to avoid any criticism and backlash. This way of representing the Prophet and his family, in particular the women of his household became the convention of early modern Ottoman art signalling a paradigm shift in traditionalist interpretation of the image of women in Islam. Through this, they represent the ideal models of chastity, virtue and piety. They became a model for the Ottoman imperial women of the *harem* in the sixteenth century to emulate through their patronage and philanthropic works.

Keywords: *Ottoman Empire, women, iconography, seclusion, harem, patronage, representation*

At the end of the 14th Century, a Mevlevi dervish who came to the palace of Sultan Berkuk, the Mamluk ruler in Cairo, undertook an important duty. At the wish of the Sultan, Mustafa, son of Yusuf, from Erzurum (in Anatolia) was to write the book *Siyer-i Nebi*, in which once again the life of the Prophet Muhammad would be invoked and the subject would once again be made into an epic. Mustafa was blind, and for that reason he was known by the epithet Darir, which means "sightless". Darir completed his book around 1388. Whatever there was known about the Prophet Muhammad was revealed in this work and composed in Ottoman Turkish. The work made use of both pre-Islamic Arabic legends and enriched with verses from the Qur'an and the *hadiths*.[1] Two hundred years later, the Ottoman Sultan Murad III (d.1595) commissioned the chief painter of the palace atelier Lütfü Abdullah to transform the Turkish epic into a visual narrative.

The first section of this study focuses on the selected illustrations from this manuscript to demonstrate the early modern Ottoman representations of Muslim women of the Prophet's household. Emulating the women of Prophet Muhammad's household, the second part of the essay looks at the symbolic connection between the women of the Prophet Muhammad's household and the Ottoman imperial women including Hürrem Sultan (wife of Süleyman the Magnificent) and his daughter Mihrimah Sultan.

Siyer-i Nebi consisting of six volumes with a total of 814 miniatures where Volumes I, II and VI are in the Topkapi Palace Museum, Volume III at the New York Public Library and Volume IV housed at the Chester Beatty Library in Dublin. Volume V together with 200 of other miniatures is missing. With limited publications available on these religious manuscripts, their representation of female agency in relation to Ottoman imperial women through the symbolism of the Prophet's ideal family need to be considered.[2] Aesthetically speaking the manuscripts deserve attention as well. The paintings introduce new styles while maintaining both traditional and classical Ottoman styles and motifs.[3] One of the problems with the miniature paintings is that there are no signatures to determine the artists. However, as Carol Fisher has shown "stylistic comparisons [...] suggest the connections with this manuscript of such court artists as Naqqaş Hasan Paşa, Lütfü Abdullah, and Osman."[4]

What has not been considered before in scholarly research through these miniature paintings is that this essay provides another interpretation by showing how the iconography of *Siyer-i Nebi* rather than legitimising the seclusion of women, subverts their absence of their physical presence in the traditionally patriarchal domain – both in seventh century Arabia of early Islam and sixteenth century Ottoman imperial court – through the Ottoman setting.

Siyer-i Nebi and the representations of Muslim women in the Prophet Muhammad's household

The manuscript provides art historians two avenues for discussion regarding the representations of early Muslim women. Firstly, the study focuses on the court painters' depictions of the women of the Prophet's household like his mother Amina, his two wives Kahdija and Aisha, and his daughter Fatima all veiled. Through the portrayals of these ladies of the early Muslim era, the artists are able to construct an image of the 'ideal' woman in Islamic society that of a pious individual. Secondly, the cementing of imperial women's role in Ottoman society in the sixteenth century was largely dependent on their Islamic piety. Although this is visually very clear through their numerous architectural patronages with their mosque complexes, the royal women had to ensure they represented the 'ideal' Muslim woman like that of the women in Prophet Muhammad's life, his wives Khadija and Aisha, and his daughter Fatima.

The imperial women's 'sacred' status as 'mothers of the believers' connecting them to the Prophet Muhammad's wives and daughter may explain the prohibition on them being visually depicted in paintings and to be seen in public in person.[5] But this religious argument becomes problematic and even contradictory when in the *Siyer-i Nebi* commissioned by Murad III, the women in Prophet Muhammad's life were clearly depicted in the miniatures, albeit without their faces. The question then remains to be asked: why weren't the Ottoman imperial women depicted like that of the women of Prophet Muhammad?

The limitation attached to this argument is that these selected paintings only constitute a very minute sample of the total 814 miniatures. It has been difficult to establish the structure of the complete miniatures as they are held in various parts of the world and in private collections, and where an entire volume is missing this adds to the arduous nature of the task.[6]

The first section of the essay focuses on the following miniature paintings: two miniatures depicting the birth of Muhammad; marriage between Muhammad and Khadija; Aisha informing Muhammad on people with infectious diseases; and Muhammad and Aisha freeing a slave. The second half of the essay looks at the representations of two women of the Ottoman imperial family as "Mothers of Believers" like Khadija and Aisha: Hürrem Sultan and her daughter, Mihrimah Sultan.

Representations of the birth of Muhammad

The birth of Muhammad miniature comes from Volume I of the *Siyer-i Nebi*. Zeren Tanındı believes that an assistant named Nakkaş Hasan Pasha [Painter Three] to the head painters Osman and Ali Nakkaş may have contributed to its creation (*Figure 1*).[7] Tanındı believes that a similar technique of dividing the architecture of the setting in the painting into three or four arched background sections is also seen in the death scene of Volume VI. The painter uses tiles to indicate the floor and the walls of the room. He uses the area under the left arch to manipulate it to suggest a "spatial vista".

Figure 1. Siyer-i Nebi, birth of Muhammad visited by angels, Istanbul, c.1595. Photograph reproduction.

The figures lean towards the centre focal area, the baby Muhammad. The figures appear to be lively and engaged as shown by the crowned and winged angels bearing gifts to the baby. The angels standing behind bring with them a silver pitcher and towel while angel kneeling presents the baby to what appears to be a tambourine heralding the arrival of al-Mustafa, the chosen-one, as his mother Amina with raised arms looks on with amazement. Although her veiled white face attracts the viewer but the raised arms, which the painter has cleverly animated, take away from her faceless representation. The glowing halo in the Eastern tradition around the baby rises toward the ceiling exemplifying his holiness. In another birth scene, perhaps by the same painter, as indicated by the arches, the ceramic lamp hanging in the centre of the middle arch and, tiled floor and walls, is dominated by the leading male figures of Mecca and two women visiting Amina to congratulate her on the birth of her son (*Figure 2*).

Figure 2. Siyer-i Nebi, another birth scene of baby Muhammad – the baby presented to his grandfather and the Meccan community, Istanbul, c.1595. Photograph reproduction.

As in the previous image, the painter similarly manipulates the left arch to emphasise spatial vista. In this scene, Amina shows her baby to his grandfather Abdul Muttalib as seen in the grey bearded figure in the blue robe. Interestingly, the baby is also presented to other members of the Meccan community both men and almost unveiled women seen in the lower left corner of the painting. Amina's presence in the midst of other males looking on here signifies Islam placing no restrictions on women being in the presence of men. Orthodox Islam would argue that the image represents pre-Islamic period where mixing of the sexes was the norm. However, the semi-veiled women where their mouths are covered depicted in the scene and the faceless mother of baby Muhammad negates that point suggesting the acceptable Ottoman cultural practices of the sixteenth century. Once again, the painter has the subjects on the left and centre of the painting leaning toward the baby as he is being presented to them.

Representation of the marriage of Muhammad and Khadija

Muhammad at age 25 married Khadija fifteen years his senior and twice divorced (*Figure 3*). As a wealthy widow who had acquired the wealth of her previous husbands it is evident that women in pre-Islamic times had been granted rights to property and wealth. She admired his character and qualities, and proposed to him, showing her independence and open mindedness in seventh century Arabia.[8]

Figure 3. Siyer-i Nebi, marriage of Muhammad and Khadija, Istanbul, c.1595. Photograph reproduction.

In the painting of the marriage of Khadija to Muhammad the wedding ceremony is taking place. Muhammad is seated at the centre wearing his green robe and the decorative turban signifying his groom status. To his left most likely is his elderly uncle Abu Talib, who brought him up since the age of six, after the death of his mother,[9] seen with his grey beard wearing a similar turban signifying his relationship to the groom. The figure standing in the bottom right of the image presenting a gift to the couple could be the uncle of Khadija, Amr ibn Asad, as her parents were deceased by this time in her life. At the wedding he stood and spoke of the virtues of Khadijah, "for we, indeed are the foremost

RENAISSANCE WOMEN

among the Arabs, and so are you [Abu Talib and his family]. No one could deny your [Khadija] virtue among the Arabs."[10] Once again the spatial vista is manipulated on the left arch, but this time there are guests who are about to enter the room to join the other guests depicted in their dark and light blue robes, suggesting that they may be Muhammad's uncles. The striking colour dominating the right section of the painting is red, as Kahdija who is sitting behind a barrier being attended by her slave away from the men, is wearing, and signifying the colour of the traditional Muslim wedding dress.

In this painting the allusions to the Ottoman context are seen two ways: sexual and place of wife. Firstly, the colour red represents the breaking of the hymen during intercourse. The woman wearing the red is the sexual agent through the reproduction process gives birth to a possible heir and she owes her status to this. This scene clearly represents the *haremlik* (private, usually for women) and *selamlik* (public, usually dominated by men) of the Topkapi Palace. Facing the viewer in a similar seated position as that of the males, the woman's assertive presence is further accentuated and reinforced through the halo. There is one similarity between Khadija and Hürrem in this scene. It is unclear whether Hürrem proposed to Süleyman, but what is clear is that she did charm him with her quick wit and humour.[11] By marrying a sultan-caliph, represented by the Prophet, the status of Haseki Hürrem has risen to that of the "mother of the believers" and her virtues like that of Khadija's cannot be denied through her pious works as will be discussed in the second sections of the essay.

Aisha informing Prophet Muhammad about infectious diseases

The next painting depicts the Prophet's other wife Aisha giving information to her husband and other people, including men and women on communicable diseases (*Figure 4*). The style of the painting is different from the previous images. The background is less stylised as is the halo of the Prophet. The colours are much drier and less vibrant as seen in the robes of the subjects, the carpets and the background arches. There is no golden glow in the halo of the Prophet as in the previous images. There is no sense of spatial vista in this painting. The background is flat, very mono-dimensional. The women are depicted without any identity as indicated by their complete covering including their hands, unlike Khadija in the marriage painting above. Here the woman wearing brown who is the closest to the Prophet represents Aisha, and is larger in size than the other women in the painting. Her and other women's presence in the company of men, considering Aisha's status as the wife of the Prophet, is significant. Aisha is known for her intelligence in Islamic history, and a warrior who challenged her rival Ali after the death of her husband. Although the size of the character of Muhammad is slightly larger than that of others including that of Aisha, there is no single central focus in the painting.

Figure 4. Siyer-i Nebi, Aisha giving information to Muhammad and other people, Istanbul, c.1595. Photograph reproduction.

Both Aisha and Prophet Muhammad occupy our attention as the important figures. Her intelligence is represented here by her informing the people with valuable knowledge about contagious diseases as the others with hands raised in prayer formation asking God for cure from such ailments. What appears here is that a woman is using her knowledge to educate the community in the presence of men. She is in charge of the whole scene. Wearing the darkest colour is indicative of this and draws our attention to her from the very beginning. Once acquainted with the context and meaning of the painting the veils on the faces of the women lose their significance and highlight the Islamic perception of the illusion of seclusion of women in society. As in the above paintings, this image too represents the Ottoman royal women especially Mihrimah Sultan who in her *vakfiye* (endowment deed) states she possessed the intelligence of Aisha; corresponded with foreign diplomats, became her father's close confidant after her mother's death, and involved in charitable works. With Nurbanu (wife of Selim II) and Safiye Sultans (wife of Murad III) using their influences on their husbands to prevent war with Venice thereby giving the Ottoman Empire an uninterrupted peace with its Mediterranean rival.[12]

Prophet Muhammad and Aisha freeing a slave

Freeing of slaves was common among the Ottoman elite. The women of the *harem* after their education was over, it was the role of the *valide* sultan (Queen Mother) to marry the girls in the *harem* to one of the sultan's pashas where the sultan oversaw the expenses of the wedding.[13] Thus, this act of manumission by the palace was a joint act between the sultan and his mother. This custom is depicted in a similar way in the miniature painting where Prophet Muhammad and his wife Aisha free the daughter of a tribal chief in the presence of onlookers, men and women (*Figure 5*).

Figure 5. Siyer-i Nebi, Muhammad and Aisha freeing a slave, Istanbul, c.1595. Photograph reproduction.

The two central figures in Figure 5 are Prophet Muhammad and Aisha. They are standing side-by-side portraying their equal status wearing green and white respectively, the former representing his prophethood and leader of the community through the colour green, the latter in her long white robe signifying her chastity and piety as one of the "Mothers of Believers" attributed to her in the Qur'an.[14] Both their hands pointing at the kneeling woman thanking them for her granting of freedom, as if to show their humility in trying to help her up that it is not necessary for her to do this. The equal status of Aisha and Prophet Muhammad in this image represent the good deed committed by both husband and wife.

Similarly, in the Ottoman context marrying slave girls of the palace demonstrated the good deed of both the mother and son. The style of this painting is similar to the first two above where vibrant, bright colours are used to depict the subjects. The central blue hill is used as a contrasting background for the important three figures, Aisha in white, Prophet Muhammad in green and the freed slave girl in red. Once again as in the above paintings the action takes place in the presence of both men and women. All the women here are unveiled. Their faces are clearly visible, expressing their somewhat mixed emotions at what is taking before them exemplified by their animated heads tilting to show empathy. Although men are in the scene, their presence is diminished by their position behind the blue hill giving them a distance from the women's space. This distance, however, does not impinge on them witnessing the event and commenting on it as seen by the two top left figures where sharp indentation of the upper part of their noses is seen. The dominance of women in this image including the good deed committed by her, similarly, exemplify the equally principal role of Ottoman imperial women in the sixteenth century.

Representations of Ottoman imperial women as 'Mothers of Believers'

The illustrations in *Siyer-i Nebi* may provide an explanation where in some miniatures women are together with men, for example at the birth of the baby Muhammad both men and almost unveiled women occupying the same space are congratulating Amina; while in others they are separated by a barrier as seen in the marriage ceremony of Muhammad and Khadija. The appropriation of seventh century historical events from Prophet Muhammad's life into the sixteenth century Ottoman setting, the paintings further reinforce this allusion of the place of imperial women, their agency in public and private.

Ottoman imperial women like Hürrem Sultan and Mihrimah Sultan have been compared to the "Mothers of the Believers" as the Qur'an describes the wives of the Prophet.[15] If the Prophet's wives were the ideal women then his daughter Fatima was the ideal daughter, which Mihrimah and other women of the court came to embody through their pious works. Her *vakfiye* of 1550 refers to the princess as the sultan's favoured daughter "Mihrimah Sultan Hanım", a "Fatima in innocence, a Khadija in chastity, an Aisha in intelligence ...and the Rabi'a of the epoch."[16] The comparisons to the Prophet's family is clearly evident and reinforcing the pious nature of the women "enabling her [Hürrem] to bring forth on the hidden virtues from behind a veiled canopy, in order that they may be known [...]."[17] It must be stated that the *vakfiyes* are composed by men to represent the 'ideal' Muslim woman as exemplified in the Qur'an and in the tradition of the Prophet. While the written word is the perceptions of males of females, the paintings on the other hand represent a different reality that may have existed in Ottoman society. Although the *vakfiyes* (endowment deeds) of the women suggest that it is through their piety that they wished to have been known as their mosques signify upholding their Islamic duty, at the same time the women "behind a veiled canopy" are challenging patriarchy to assert their authority by demonstrating that it is also the right of the woman as ordained by God to accomplish good deeds like their male counterparts and through these acts to inform the public of their presence. From a feminist perspective, Luce Irigaray argues the women of the *harem* assign to the feminine by resorting to "mimicry", thereby challenging their subordination through good charitable works.[18] This is not to say that their intentions were not for the sake of faith, but that their intentions were twofold. These representations of women in religious iconography thus demonstrate their equal status in society sitting and sharing the same public space as men, which challenges the traditionalist interpretation of their passive role from behind the 'veil'.

Haseki (Hürrem Sultan): Süleyman's 'Queen' and 'the benevolent dame'

Perhaps no other concubine received as much attention as that of Hürrem. Her title as Haseki (the favourite who bore the sultan a child) of Süleyman added to her status. But added to this her marriage to Süleyman would promote her ascendancy among the ruling elite even further. Orientalist literature on the Ottoman society, accounts are presented either with distortion or with exaggeration concerning women. Orientalist discourse especially the seraglio (palace) and the harem depict women as sexual objects who are not entitled to any rights in society. In fact, there were many women of the imperial family who were among those who founded mosques, hospitals, schools, public kitchens, libraries, care houses for the widowed and orphans through the *vakf* (charitable) institution. Women commissioning such works through the *vakf* institution shows that the imperial women and also other women at large could entitle themselves to property and had a crucial say in economic life. "In a land survey conducted in Istanbul in 1546, 913 of the 2517 *vakfs* in the city were instituted by women" cementing her role as an ideal Muslim woman of her day like that of the Prophet's wives.[19] Two such women included the wife and daughter of Süleyman, Hürrem Sultan who had the official title Haseki Sultan being his legitimately wedded wife and longer his slave, and Mihrimah Sultan respectively (*Figures 5a-b*).

Figures 5a, 5b. Left, sixteenth century Ottoman portrait of Sultan Süleyman by court painter Nakkas Osman. Right, late 19th century representation of Haseki Hürrem Sultan, anonymous. Photograph reproductions.

Hated by the people for having supposedly bewitched the sultan to marry her and for plotting the murder of Prince Mustafa, the heir to the throne, Hürrem Sultan, however, left her architectural imprint on the main urban centres of the empire: Istanbul and Edirne; and three Holy Cities of Islam (Mecca, Medina, Jerusalem). Her building programs including mosques, soup kitchens and women's refuge centres can be read as trying to improve her public image as a philanthropist queen devoted to the welfare of Ottoman subjects. Thus, her self-representation lies between the rumours spread about her and her architectural monuments spread throughout the corners of the empire.

Hürrem was constrained by the codes of decorum to negotiate her contested unprecedented status in Ottoman society of the sixteenth century. This self-representation is thus reflected publicly through visually restrained monuments unlike the complexes of her daughter Mihrimah Sultan and daughter-in-law Nurbanu Sultan. Her complex therefore was not representative of its monumentality or stylistic originality but the richly endowed charitable services they provided the population. This can be read in two ways: first depicting herself as a pious Muslim monarch; and secondly remedying her negative image in the eyes of her subjects. This was not lost on Ottoman historians in the 1590s when Talikzade almost eulogises Hürrem as the ideal Muslim woman of the age:

> One of the firm pillars supporting the sultanate of his noble highness was his illustrious, canonically lawful wife's world-nourishing, potent magnanimity and the flourishing harvest of her benevolence ... she built countless ... masjids, Friday mosques, bath-houses, shops, convents for the poor dervishes, waterworks, and bridges... In this exalted and fortunate state she left behind numerous and countless praiseworthy memorials. The Lady of Time has not see such an abundantly benevolent dame.[20]

Praising her countless works Talikzade compares her to those of the celebrated Abbasid Queen Zubayda and her monuments. Thus, seeing his perspective on Hürrem in the 1590s reinforces the many projects the palace ateliers were working on at this time under Murad III. In her *vakfiye* and the title deed dated 1560 mention her as "the Zubayda of the age".[21]

The mosque Sinan built for Haseki (Hürrem) Sultan in Istanbul in 1539 was one of his earliest works for an imperial woman after having being appointed as chief architect of the empire. In the course of time, it has been enlarged by Süleyman to include a madrasah, a primary school, an imaret and a hospital, making it the "largest social amenities centre in the area" (*Figure 6*).[22]

The location of the mosque is rather symbolic. Situated near the Avratpazarı (female slave market) on the ancient Forum of Arcadius, ancient Roman discourse juxtaposed with the Ottoman narrative (*Figure 7*). The ancient column incidentally was also known as the Maiden's or Woman's column. Sixteenth century traveller John Sanderson describes the area as "the markett place of women, for thether come to sell thier wourks and wares."[23]

Figure 6. Haseki Hürrem Hospital in Istanbul, signifying Hürrem's benevolence and charitable foundation. Photograph by Metin Mustafa, December, 2014.

Figure 7. Haseki Hürrem complex built at the site of Avratpazarı to help despondent women of the day. Photograph by Metin Mustafa, December, 2014.

A 17th century miniature from Cicogna Codex manuscript shows both men and women at the site with the Haseki Mosque in the background (*Figure 8*).[24] With the symbolism of the location perhaps "Süleyman the

Magnificent was displaying a certain delicacy towards his wife."[25] This can be read as someone like Hürrem Sultan who came to the *harem* as a slave and rose to be the Queen of the empire. Her clemency for slaves, like the Prophet's wife Aisha, is thus seen in her *vakf*. Her charitable endowment catered to buy shoes and slippers for the needy children slaves.[26] Symbolically the visual metaphor of the mosque highlights the meritocratic system of the empire – that not only men slaves rose to become Grand Viziers but women slaves too reached high positions even to legally wed a sultan and have him remain in a monogamous relationship with her.

Figure 8: Avratpazarı Market place, 17th century Istanbul with the Haseki Mosque in the background. Photograph reproduction.

According to the queen's *vakf* specifications the elementary school teacher had to be affectionate like a father, the sheykh of the hospice had to greet needy visitors with kind words and refrain from derogatory comments. The doctors of the hospital had to converse with patients like affectionate friends using tender words which are "sweeter than the fountain of paradise."[27] Hürrem was most likely concerned with the psychology of the students and patients because of her frail, hunchbacked son Jihangir and the gout-stricken husband. Income was generated from the selling of fruits and flowers grown in the garden from the complex, which Hürrem used to free slaves, like in the painting depiction of Aisha and Prophet Muhammad above, with the surplus funds of her endowment. Hürrem's mosque complex became a "massive welfare project noteworthy for the variety of public services its dependencies provided to the poor and needy, was the most monumental foundation established by a woman in that era."[28] Her charitable works not only bolstered her pious standing in the empire, but also bolstered her sultan-husband's caliph status as the sole leader of the Sunni Islamic world.

Mihrimah Sultan: "Fatima in innocence, a Khadija in chastity, an Aisha in intelligence and the Rabi'a of the epoch"

Mihrimah Sultan, whose name means sun and moon, was the most privileged lady of the court (*Figure 9*). Like her mother Hürrem's philanthropic works, Süleyman's daughter not only left her mark on Istanbul's skyline, but also a legacy of charitable works through her mosque complexes.

Sinan built two mosque complexes for her, one during her twenties as the loving and only daughter of Süleyman and the other as the widowed princess and the not-so-beloved sister of Selim II because of her support for her other brother Beyazid for the throne. Her enormous wealth was doubled by the death of her husband Rustem Pasha who left her an annual income of thirty million *aspers* (Ottoman currency) which gave her a daily stipend of 600 *aspers*, "the highest sum awarded to any princess in the classical age."[29]

Figure 9. Imaginary portrait of Mihrimah Sultan, daughter of Süleyman the Magnificent and Hürrem Sultan by the Florentine artist Cristofano dell'Altissimo c.1552 /1557 for Cosimo de Medici. "Dressed in a plain brown gown with floral motifs, the figure wears a tall headdress ornate with expensive stones. She is set against a dark background upon which are the following inscriptions on the upper left and upper right corners, respectively: 'Cameria Solimani Imparator Filia' (Cameria, Daughter of Sultan Süleyman) and 'Rostanis Bassae Vxor 1541' (Wife of Rüstem Pasha, 1541). It is highly probable that the date inscribed here does not indicate the date on which the work was executed. It can be assumed that the date and the inscription found on virtually all of the similar portraits by different artists repeat a tradition initiated by the first original portrait." Pera Museum, Istanbul, Turkey. Photograph reproduction.

Mihrimah Sultan became the only royal woman to have two mosques built in her name: one at Üsküdar on the shoreline of the Bosphorus with two minarets as she was permitted to do being a royal princess, and the other at Edirnekapı, near the Edirne Gate on the city walls, on the very opposite side of the city in the European quarter (*Figures 10-11*). This article looks at the former structure to demonstrate her charitable characteristics. Mihrimah's patronage shows her unique status in Süleyman's family as the ideal pious daughter.

Figures 10 and 11. Left, Mihrimah Sultan Camii at Üsküdar; below, Edirnekapı Camii of Mihrimah Sultan. Photographs by Metin Mustafa, December, 2014.

Located on the Asian side of the Bosphorus, Üsküdar was on the outside of the political and administrative centre of the Istanbul in the sixteenth century. The town was an active trade route, which was passing through Asia Minor and going to the Caucasus and Iran. The town was also the starting point of the hajj pilgrimage journey where every year pilgrims were sent to Mecca with ceremonies from Üsküdar.[30] Thus, the location was an ideal place to demonstrate the piety of the princess to the masses and presenting her as the ideal daughter of a universal monarch, like that of the Prophet's daughter Fatima. This first mosque was built near the boat landing between 1543-1548. At this location was also the garden palace of the princess where she could easily attend prayers. On the inscription panel above the portal of the mosque states it was built by "Hanım Sultan", (Lady Sultan), the daughter of Süleyman I.[31] The *vakf* records of the complex include a mosque, a madrasah, a guesthouse, a caravanserai functioning as a stable and a hospice (*imaret*) which consisted of a kitchen, a pantry and a storage and an elementary school.[32] Contemporary historian Ramazanzade Mehmed's chronicle in 1590 describes the mosque in the following words:

> Her Highness, the foundress of pious foundations and the bestower of good works, the daughter of His Highness the world-protecting sultan ... built in Üsküdar as an expression of her pure intentions a Friday mosque ... an embellished mosque that is a gathering place for piety and worship, a madrasa, a generous hospice, an unequalled elementary school to which a teacher was appointed to instruct children with the recitation and chanting of the Koran, and several independent chambers and rooms were distinguished and poor guests are given abundant food in banquets day and night, treated respectfully so that they might enjoy repose, tranquillity, and pleasure. In the year 950 (1543-44).[33]

The mosque providing the inhabitants of Istanbul daily food servings and education for the children further reinforcing her *vakfiye* statement: "Fatima in innocence, a Khadija in chastity, an Aisha in intelligence ... and the Rabi'a of the epoch."[34] According to Necipoğlu, the princess ensured during Friday sermons at her mosque, the righteous imam offer prayers to the souls of the prophets and saints, "[... especially to the Prophet's daughter Fatima, and to other Ottoman sultans" symbolically connecting herself to the early Muslim "Mothers of the Believers" and cementing her legacy as the ideal pious daughter of Sultan Süleyman.[35]

Conclusively, the representations of Muslim women in early modern Ottoman manuscript the *Siyer-i Nebi* demonstrate the role of imperial women as active participants in sixteenth century Ottoman society. As the manuscript was intended for the imperial family viewing only, the artist's visual depictions of the women of Prophet Muhammad's household in painting signal artistic freedom to represent these women for the Ottoman elite audience. In this way, the cleverly selected scenes from the Prophet's everyday life with his family became exemplary role model to emulate for the imperial women like Hürrem Sultan and Mihrimah Sultan, among others. Such depictions and actions taken by the imperial women also served to augment the political status of the sultan throughout his realm and beyond.

Drawing on their Islamic legacy, the Ottoman artists utilised the events from the life of Prophet Muhammad to demonstrate in the manuscript *Siyer-i Nebi* a connection of between the imperial women of the Sultan Süleyman and those of Prophet Muhammad's wife Aisha and daughter, Fatima. As "Mothers of the Believers", the imperial women represented an historical connection between the Prophet's family tradition and that of his own to further support his claim to the title of caliph - Leader of the Islamic *ummah* (community). Additionally, the Ottoman imperial women resorting to patriarchal mimicry using architectural works further signalled their equal status and presence in the early modern Ottoman society.

Bibliography

Barkan, Ömer Lutfi and Ekrem Hakkı Ayverdi, eds. *Istanbul Vakıfları Tahrir Defteri, 953 (1546) Tarihli.* Istanbul: Istanbul Fetih Cemiyeti, 1970.

Blair, S. S and Jonathan M. Bloom. *The Art and Architecture of Islam, 1250-1800.* New Haven and London: Yale University Press), 1996.

Dursteler, E. R. *Venetians in Constantinople: Nation, Identity, And Coexistence in the Early Modern Mediterranean.* Baltimore: The John Hopkins University Press, 2006.

Düzbakar, Ömer. 'Charitable Women And Their Pious Foundations In The Ottoman Empire: The Hospital of the Senior Mother, Nurbanu Valide Sultan.' Uludağ University, Faculty of Arts and Sciences, Department of History, Bursa, 2006. Accessed March 19, 2014. https://www.ishim.net/ishimj/910 JISHIM%20NO.10%20PDF/03.pdf.

Efendi, E. *Osmanlılarda Töre ve Törenler*, edited by Yavuz Ercan. Istanbul: Tercüman, 1979.

BIBLIOGRAPHY

Fisher, C. C. 'A Reconstruction of the Pictorial Cycle of the "Siyar-i Nabī" of Murād III.' *Ars Orientalis*, Vol. 14 (1984): 75-94, Freer Gallery of Art and University of Michigan. Accessed April 16, 2014. http://www.jstor.org/discover/10.2307/4629330?

Goodwin, G. *A History of Ottoman Architecture*. London, UK: Thames and Hudson, 1971.

Goodwin, G. *The Private World of Ottoman Women*. London: Saqi Essentials, 2006.

Haylamaz, R. *Khadija: The First Muslim and the Wife of the Prophet Muhammad*. Translated by Hülya Coşar. New Jersey: Tughra Books, 2010.

Irigaray, L. *The Sex Which Is Not*. Translated by Catherine Porter and Caroline Burke. Ithaca, New York: Cornell University Press, 1985.

Kuban, D. *Istanbul Yazıları*. Istanbul: Yapı Endustrisi Merkezi Yayınları, 1998.

Kürkçüoğlu, K. E. *Süleymaniye Vakfiyesi*. Ankara: Vakıflar Umum Müdürlüğü, 1962.

Kuban, D. *Ottoman Architecture*. Suffolk: Antique Collectors Club Distributors, 2010.

Mazlum, D. *Dünden Bügüne Istanbul Ansikplopedisi*, vol. 7. Istanbul: Tarih Vakfı, 1993.

Necipoğlu, G. *The Age of Sinan, The Age of Sinan: Architectural Culture in the Ottoman Empire*. London: Reaktion Books, reprinted 2011.

Peirce, L. P. *The Imperial Harem: Women and Sovereignty in the Ottoman Empire*. New York: Oxford University Press, 1993.

'Siyer-i Nebi: The Life of the Prophet.' *Antika: The Turkish Journal Of Collectable Art*, 15 (1986). Accessed April 13, 2014. http://www.ee.-bilkent.edu.tr/~history/Ext/prophet.html

BIBLIOGRAPHY

Stephan, St H. 'An Endowment Deed of Khaseki Sultan, Dated the 24th May, 1552.' *Quarterly of the Department of Antiquities in Palestine* 10 (1944): 170-94.

Talikizade, *Sehname-i Hümayun*. Istanbul: Topkapi Sarayi Muzesi.

Taşkıran, N. *Hasekinin Kitabı*. Istanbul: Haseki Hastanesi Kalkındırma Derneği, 1972.

Notes

1. RENAISSANCE WOMEN'S PATRONAGE - A COMPARATIVE READING OF EARLY MODERN WOMEN'S PATRONAGE IN ITALY AND OTTOMAN ISTANBUL

1. See Leslie P. Peirce, "Gender and Sexual Propriety in Ottoman Royal Women's Patronage," in *Women, Patronage and Self-Representation in Islamic Societies*, edited by D. Fairchild Ruggles, 53-68 (New York: State University of New York Press, 2000); also see Lucienne Thys-Senocak, "The Yeni Valide Mosque Complex of Eminönü, Istanbul (1597-1665): Gender and Vision in Ottoman Architecture," in *Women, Patronage and Self-Representation in Islamic Societies*, edited by D. Fairchild Ruggles, 69-90 (New York: State University of New York Press, 2000).
2. D. Fairchild Ruggles, "Vision and Power," in *Women, Patronage and Self-Representation in Islamic Societies*. New York: State University of New York Press, 2000), 5.
3. Luce Irigaray, *The Sex Which Is Not*, trans. by Catherine Porter and Caroline Burke (Ithaca, New York: Cornell University Press, 1985), 76.
4. Ibid., 76.
5. Ibid., 84.
6. Debra Coleman, "Introduction," in *Architecture and Feminism*, edited by Debra Coleman, Elizabeth Denza, and Carol Henderson (New York, Princeton Architectural Press, 1996), xii.
7. Ibid., xii.
8. Elizabeth Grosz, "Women, *Chora*, Dwelling," in *Postmodern Cities and Spaces*, ed. Sophie Watson and Katherine Gibson (Oxford, Blackwell Publishers, 1995), 47.
9. Ibid., 55.
10. Coleman, "Introduction," xiv.
11. S. Chojnacki, *Women and Men in Renaissance Venice: Twelve Essays on Patrician Society* (Baltimore and London: The John Hopkins University Press, 2000), 6.
12. Ibid., 3-6.
13. Suraiya Faroqhi, *Subjects of the Sultan: Culture and Daily Life in the Ottoman Empire* (London, UK: IB Tauris, 2010), 113.
14. Chojnacki, *Women and Men in Renaissance Venice*, 6.
15. Margaret King, *Women of the Renaissance* (Chicago: University of Chicago Press, 1991), 48.
16. Ibid., 49.
17. Catherine King, *Renaissance Women Patrons: Wives and Widows in Italy c. 1300-1550* (UK: Manchester University Press, 1998), 48.
18. Ibid., 48.
19. Faroqhi, *Subjects of the Sultan*, 112-113.
20. King, *Women of the Renaissance*, 49.
21. Cited in Ibid., 50.

NOTES

22. Ibid., 52.
23. Ibid., 64.
24. Iris Origo, *The Merchant of Prato: Francesco di Marco Datini* (London: Jonathan Cape, 1957), 339-40.
25. King, *Women of the Renaissance*, 55
26. Ibid., 55.
27. Ibid., 55.
28. Ibid., 55.
29. Ibid., 56.
30. Ibid., 56.
31. See A. M. Roberts, "Chiara Gambacorta of Pisa as Patroness of the Arts," in *Creative Women in Medieval and Early Modern Italy*, ed. E.A. Matter and J. Coakley (Philadelphia: University of Philadelphia Press), 120-154.
32. Ibid., 120-154.
33. G. Radke, "Nuns and their Art: The Case of San Zaccaria in Renaissance Venice", *Renaissance Quarterly*, 54 (2001): 442.
34. Ibid., 443.
35. For more see Mustafa, *The Ottoman Renaissance*.
36. Filiz Cağman and Engin Yenal, eds., *Topkapı: The Palace of Felicity*, trans. Robert Bragner (Istanbul: Ertuğ & Kölük, 1992), 109.
37. Irvin Cemil Shick, "The Harem as Gendered Space and the Spatial Reproduction of Gender," In *Harem Histories: Envisioning Places and Living Spaces*, ed. Marilyn Booth (London: Duke University Press, 2010), 80.
38. Cristoforo Valier cited in John Freely, *Inside the Seraglio: Private Lives of the Sultans in Istanbul* (England: Viking, 1999), 108.
39. Leslie Peirce, *The Imperial Harem: Women and Sovereignty in the Ottoman Empire* (New York: Oxford University Press, 1993), 8.
40. Katherine A. McIver, *The Sixteenth Century Journal* 27, 2 (1996): 628, review of *Creative Women in Medieval and Early Modern Italy: A Religious and Artistic Renaissance*, ed. E.A. Matter and J. Coakley (Philadelphia: University of Philadelphia Press), Book Review, DOI: 10.2307/2544244.
41. See Roberts, *Creative Women in Medieval and Early Modern Italy*, 120-154.
42. "The prophet is closer to the believers than their own selves, and his wives are their mothers." (Qur'an, Chapter 33; verse 6) This Surah (chapter 33) establishes the dignity and position of the Holy Prophet's wives, who had a special mission and responsibility as Mothers of the Believers. They were not to be like ordinary women: they had to instruct women in spiritual matters, visit and minister to those who were ill or in distress, and do other kindly offices in aid of the Prophet's mission. This may explain the prohibition on the depiction of Ottoman royal women in paintings. See A. Yusuf Ali translation of the Qur'an.
43. Qur'an: 33:6.
44. In their *vakfiye* documents, Mihrimah Sultan, her mother Hürrem and her aunt Shah Sultan have been compared to the mystic Sufi woman, Rabi'a from Basra (d.801). Cited in Esad Efendi, *Osmanlılarda Töre ve Törenler*, ed. Yavuz Ercan (Istanbul: Baki, 1979), 3.
45. St. H. Stephan, "An Endowment Deed of Haseki Sultan, Dated the 24th May, 1552," *Quarterly of the Department of Antiquities in Palestine*, 10 (1994): 170-94.
46. Stephan, St. H. "An Endowment Deed of Haseki Sultan," 170-94.
47. Deniz Mazlum, *Dünden Bügüne Istanbul Ansiklopedisi*, vol. 7 (Istanbul: Kültür Bakanlığı ve Tarih Vakfı Yurt Yayınları Ortak Yayını, 1994), 344-45.

NOTES

48. Doğan Kuban, *Istanbul Yazıları* (Istanbul: Yapı Endustrisi Merkezi Yayınları, 1998), 97. Mihrimah was known as 'Hanım Sultan' (Lady Sultan) whereas her mother Hürrem as 'Haseki Sultan' because she never became the Valide as she died in 1558, before her son Selim II ascended the throne in 1566.
49. Godfrey Goodwin, *A History of Ottoman Architecture* (London, UK: Thames and Hudson, 1971), 213.
50. Jale Erzen, *Sinan: Ottoman Architect, an Aesthetic Analysis* (Ankara: Middle East Technical University, Faculty of Architecture, 2004), 42.
51. Ruggles, "Vision and Power: An Introduction,".4.
52. Goodwin, *A History of Ottoman Architecture*, 214.
53. For more on this see Tülay Artan, "Boğaziçi'nin Çehresini Değiştiren Soylu Kadınlar ve Sultanefendi Sarayları," *Istanbul Dergisi* III (1992): 106-118.
54. Susan A. Skilliter, "Three Letters from the Ottoman 'Sultana' Safiye to Queen Elizabeth I," *Oriental Studies 3* (1965): 119-57.
55. Gülru Necipoğlu, *The Age of Sinan: Architectural Culture in the Ottoman Empire* (London: Reaktion Books, 2005), 311.
56. Ibid., 311.
57. Doğan Kuban, *Ottoman Architecture* (Suffolk, UK: Antique Collectors Club Distributors, 2010), 276.
58. Necipoğlu, *The Age of Sinan,* 311.
59. Ibid., 300.
60. Susan Skilliter, "The Letters of the Venetian 'Sultana' Nur Banu and Her *Kira to Venice,"* in *Studia Turcologica Memoriae Alexii Bombaci Dicata,* eds. by Gallotta and U. Marazzi (Naples: Herder, 1982), 515; also see Peirce, *The Imperial Harem,* 92.
61. Paolo Contarini, Diario del viaggio da Venezia a Constantinopoli (1580), Venice, 1856, cited in Necipoğlu, *Age of Sinan,* 281; also see *Encyclopedia of Islam: New Edition Vol. 8* (New York: Brill, 1998), 124.
62. Ibid.,124.
63. Cited in Peirce, *The Imperial Harem,* 222-23.
64. Ibid., 222-23.
65. Pınar Kayaalp, *The Empress Nurbanu and Ottoman Politics in the Sixteenth Century: Building the Atık Valide* (New York: Routledge, 2018), i.
66. See Aslı Sancar, *Ottoman Women, Ottoman Women: Myth and Reality* (New Jersey: The Light, Inc., 2007), 116; also see Kayaalp, *The Empress Nurbanu,* ii.
67. Pınar Kayaalp, "Vakfiye and Inscriptions: An Interpretation of the Written Records of the Atik Valide Mosque Complex," *International Journal of Islamic Architecture* vol. 1, 2 (2012): 301-324, accessed September, 23, 2015, http://dx.doi.org/10.1386/ijia.1.2.300_1
68. Ibid., 312.
69. The foundations for her mosque were laid in 1571 and continued after her death in 1583.
70. Ibrahim Hakkı Konyalı, *Mimar Koca Sinan'ın Eserleri* (Istanbul: Ülkü Basımevi, 1950), 80.
71. Necipoğlu, *The Age of Sinan,* 286.
72. Kuban, *Ottoman Architecture,* 339.
73. Necipoğlu, *The Age of Sinan,* 288.
74. Evliya Çelebi, *Seyahatname* vol. 1 (Istanbul: Devlet Basımevi 1896-1938), 473-476.
75. Kuban, *Ottoman Architecture,* 340.
76. Contarini cited in Ömer Düzbakar, "Charitable Women And Their Pious Foundations In The Ottoman Empire: The Hospital of the Senior Mother, Nurbanu Valide

NOTES

Sultan," Uludağ University: Faculty of Arts and Sciences, Department of History, Bursa, Turkey, 2006, 14.
77. Kayaalp, *The Empress Nurbanu*, iii.
78. Qur'an: 33:6.
79. For more see Irigaray, *The Sex Which Is Not*.
80. Wife of Sultan Ahmet I (1603-1617), Mother of Murad IV (1623-1640) and Ibrahim (1640-1648).
81. The mosque built by Mahpeyker Kösem Sultan between 1638-1640.
82. Bernardo Ricci Armani, "The Şakirin Mosque, 15 December, 2012", accessed August 14, 2015, http://ricci-armani.com/sakirin-mosque-istanbul/
83. For more on the symbolism of the tulip in Ottoman art see Mustafa, *The Ottoman Renaissance*, Chapter 6, "Ottoman Fine Arts: Word of God, Art of Man," 131-172.
84. For more on sixteenth century Ottoman Renaissance mosques see Mustafa, *The Ottoman Renaissance*, Chapter 5, "Ottoman Architecture: Surpassing the Past," 97-130.
85. For more on this see Qur'an 53:14; also see Essay V, "From Ottoman Bursa to Timurid Herat," in The forthcoming book by Metin Mustafa, *Essays: The Ottoman Renaissance and the Early Modern World, 1400-1699*.
86. Zehra Rizani, "The Woman Behind the Sakirin Mosque" in *Altmuslimah*, last modified May 27, 2009, accessed August 14, 2015, http://www.altmuslimah.com/b/mca/3090. For more see Carla Power, "Updating the Mosque for the 21st Century," *TIME Magazine*, April 2, 2009.
87. See Irigaray, *The Sex Which Is Not*.

2. NEGOTIATING GENDER IN THE EARLY MODERN PERIOD - THE ILLUSION OF SECLUSION AND THE METAPHORS OF OTTOMAN IMPERIAL WOMEN'S SOVEREIGNTY

1. See Doğan Kuban, *Ottoman Architecture* (Suffolk: Antique Collectors Club Distributors, 2010); Gülru Necipoğlu, *The Age of Sinan Architectural Culture in the Ottoman Empire* (London: Reaktion Books, 2005); Godfrey Goodwin, *A History of Ottoman Architecture*. London, UK: Thames and Hudson, 1971.
2. Eisenman cited in Mary McLeod, "Everyday and 'Other' Spaces," in *Architecture and Feminism*, Eds. Debra Coleman, Elizabeth Denza, and Carol Henderson (New York: Princeton Architectural Press, 1996), 1-2.
3. Lucienne Thys-Senocak, *Ottoman Women Builder: The Architectural Patronage of Hadice Turhan Sultan* (Vermont: Ashgate, 2006), 4.
4. Irvin Cemil Schick, "The Harem as Gendered Space and the Spatial Reproduction of Gender," in *Harem Histories: Envisioning Places and Living Spaces*, ed. Marilyn Booth, (London: Duke University Press, 2010), 80.
5. See M.W. Ferguson, M. Quilligan, N. J. Vickers, eds., *Rewriting the Renaissance: The Discourses of Sexual Difference in Early Modern Europe* (Chicago, University of Chicago Press, 1986).
6. Luce Irigaray, *The Sex Which Is Not*, Trans. by Catherine Porter and Caroline Burke (Ithaca, New York: Cornell University Press, 1985), 76.
7. Ibid., 76.
8. Ibid., 84.

NOTES

9. Ibid., 132.
10. Coleman, "Introduction," in *Architecture and Feminism*, xii.
11. Ibid., xii.
12. Elizabeth Grosz, "Women, *Chora*, Dwelling" in *Postmodern Cities and Spaces*, ed. Sophie Watson and Katherine Gibson (Oxford: Blackwell Publishers, 1995), 47.
13. Ibid., 55.
14. Coleman, "Introduction," in *Architecture and Feminism*, xiv.
15. Nicole Pohl, *Women, Space, Utopia, 1600-1800* (Burlington: Ashgate Publishing Company, 2006), 141.
16. Leslie Peirce, "Beyond Harem Walls: Ottoman Royal Women and the Exercise of Power," in *Gendered Domains: Rethinking Public and Private in Women's History*, ed. Dorothy O. Helly and Susan M. Reverby (New York: Cornell University Press, 1992), 9.
17. Mary McLeod, "Everyday and 'Other' Spaces" in Debra Coleman, Elizabeth Denza, and Carol Henderson, *Architecture and Feminism* (New York: Princeton Architectural Press, 1996), 1-2.
18. Eisenman, cited in McLeod, "Everyday and 'Other' Spaces", 2.
19. Ibid., 3.
20. For more see Edward W. Soja, *Thirdspace* (Malden, Mass.: Blackwell, 1996).
21. For more see Anthony Vidler, *The Architectural Uncanny: Essays in the Modern Unhomely* (Cambridge: The MIT Press, 1992).
22. Michel Foucault, *Architecture/Mouvement/Continuité*, October, 1984; "Des Espace Autres", March 1967, translated from the French by Jay Miskowiec, accessed March 22, 2014, http://web.mit.edu/allanmc/www/foucault1.pdf, 7.
23. See J. Derrida, *Writing and Difference*, trans. A. Bass (London & New York: Routledge, 1978), 75.
24. Ebru Boyar and Kate Fleet, eds., *Ottoman Women in Public Space* (Leiden: Brill, 2016), 1.
25. Yvonne J. Seng, "Invisible Women: Residents of Early Sixteenth-Century Istanbul," in *Women in the Medieval Islamic World: Power, Patronage, and Piety*, ed. Gavin R. G. Hambly (New York: St. Martin's Press, 1998), 241-268.
26. Aslı Sancar, *Ottoman Women: Myth and Reality* (New Jersey: The light, Inc., 2007), 38.
27. Kösem Mahpeyker Sultan was the wife of Sultan Ahmet I (1603-1617). Turhan Hatice Sultan (c.1627-1683) was the first *kadın* or *haseki* of Sultan Ibrahim I.
28. Leslie Peirce, "Domesticating Sexuality: Harem Culture in Ottoman Imperial Law," in *Harem Histories: Envisioning Places and Living Spaces*, ed. Marilyn Booth (London: Duke University Press, 2010), 104-135. Also see Ilhan Aksit, *The Mystery of the Ottoman Harem* (Istanbul: Aksit Kültür Ve Turizm Yayıncıl, 2005).
29. Thys-Senocak, *Ottoman Women Builder*, 15.
30. Leila Ahmed, "Western Ethnocentrism and Perceptions of the Harem," *Feminist Studies* 8, no. 3 (1982), accessed February 23, 2015, http://www.jstor.org/, 522-523.
31. John Freely, *Inside the Seraglio: Private Lives of the Sultans in Istanbul* (London: Penguin Books Ltd., 1999), 72.
32. Fredrick Millingen, "The Circassian Slaves and the Sultan's Harem," *Journal of the Anthropological Society of London* 8 (1870), accessed September 23, 2015, http://www.jstor.org/, cxvii.
33. Schick, "The Harem as Gendered Space and the Spatial Reproduction of Gender," 70.
34. Leslie P. Peirce. *The Imperial Harem: Women and Sovereignty in the Ottoman Empire* (New York: Oxford University Press, 1993), 7.

35. Peirce, "Beyond Harem Walls," 45.
36. Peirce, *The Imperial Harem*, 188.
37. Ibid., 248.
38. For more see *Embassy to Constantinople: The Travels of Lady Mary Wortley Montagu*, ed. Christopher Pick, with an introduction by Dervla Murphy (London: Century, 1988).
39. Philippe Du Fresne-Canaye, *Le Voyage du Levant de Philippe du Fresne-Canaye, 1573*, ed. M. H. Houser (London: British Library, 2011), 120-121.
40. See Irigaray, *The Sex Which Is Not*, 76.
41. Peirce, *Imperial Harem*, 188.
42. Evliya Çelebi, *Seyahatname*, IV, eds., Yücel Dağli and Seyit Ali Kahraman (Istanbul: Yapı Kredi Yayınları, 2001), 361; also see Ergin, "Ottoman royal women's spaces: the acoustic dimension," 95.
43. William Camden, *History of the Most Renowned and Victorious Princess Elizabeth* (London: E. Flesher for Charles Harper and John Amery, 1675), 14.
44. Anne Somerset, *Elizabeth I* (London: Phoenix Giant, 1998), 58.
45. A. L. Rowse, "The Coronation of Queen Elizabeth", *History Today* 3 (1953), accessed May 22, 2015, http://www.historytoday.com/al-rowse/coronation-queen-elizabeth#sthash.k2V6Uhff.dpuf; also see A.L. Rowse, *The England of Elizabeth* (London: Palgrave, 2003), 53, 284.
46. Selaniki Mustafa Efendi, *Tarih-i Selaniki* (Michigan: University of Michigan Library, 1989), 1: 140-41.
47. Ibid., 140-41.
48. J. Woodward, *The Theatre of Death: The ritual management of royal funerals in Renaissance England, 1570-1625* (Woodbridge: Boydell Press, 1997), 87.
49. For a more detailed account of *valide* sultan's role refer to: Aslı Sancar, *Ottoman Women*; Salih Gülen, *The Ottoman Sultans: Mighty Guests of the Throne*, trans. Emrah Şahin (New York: Blue Dome Press, 2010); Thys-Senocak, *Ottoman Women Builders*; Peirce, "Beyond Harem Walls".
50. See Derin Terzioğlu, "The Imperial Circumcision Festival of 1582: An Interpretation," *Muqarnas* 12 (1995): 84-100. Also see Stephane Yerasimos, "The Imperial Procession: Recreating a World's Order," in *Surname-i Vehbi*, accessed July 3, 2015, http://web.archive.org/web/20091025054327/http://geocities.com/surnamei_vehbi/yerasimos.html
51. D. Fairchild Ruggles, "Vision and Power: An Introduction," in *Women, Patronage and Self-Representation in Islamic Societies*, ed. D. Fairchild Ruggles (New York: State University of New York Press, 2000), 5.
52. For more see Ibid., 69-90.
53. Boyar and Fleet, *Ottoman Women in Public Space*, 11. Also see Nina Ergin, "Ottoman royal women's spaces: the acoustic dimension," *Journal of Women's History* 26, 1 (2014): 89.
54. Hans Belting, *Florence and Baghdad: Renaissance Art and Arab Science*, trans. by Deborah Lucas Schneider (Cambridge: The Belknap Press of Harvard University Press, 2011), 210.
55. Nurhan Atasoy and Robert Bragner, *1582 Surname-i Hümayun: An Imperial Celebration* (Istanbul: Koçbank, 1997), 22.
56. For more on this see Belting, *Florence and Baghdad*, 252-260.
57. Ibid., 255.
58. Ibid., 260.
59. Thys-Senocak, *Ottoman Women Builder*, 9.

NOTES

60. Lucienne Thys-Senocak, "The Yeni Valide Mosque Complex of Eminönü Istanbul (1597-1665): Gender and Vision in Ottoman Architecture," in *Women, Patronage and Self-Representation in Islamic Societies*, ed. D. Fairchild Ruggles (New York: State University of New York Press, 2000), 83.
61. Ibid., 83-84.

3. TWO QUEENS, THREE LETTERS AND THREE GIFTS - METAPHORS OF THE VISUAL LANGUAGE OF FEMALE SOVEREIGNTY IN THE EARLY MODERN PERIOD

1. Marina Luschenko, "The Correspondence of Ottoman Women during the Early Modern Period (16th– 18th Centuries): Overview on the Current State of Research, Problems, and Perspectives," in *Women's Memory: The Problem of Sources*, eds. D. Fatma Türe and Birsen T. Keşoğlu (Newcastle: Cambridge Scholars Publishing, 2011), 66.
2. Bernadette Andrea, *Women and Islam in Early Modern English Literature* (Cambridge: Cambridge University Press, 2007), 2.
3. Ibid., 9.
4. Ibid., 9.
5. Ibid., 13.
6. Luce Irigaray, *The Sex Which Is Not,* trans. Catherine Porter and Caroline Burke (Ithaca, New York: Cornell University Press, 1985), 76.
7. Ibid., 76.
8. Ibid., 84.
9. Ibid., 132.
10. Elizabeth Grosz, "Women, *Chora*, Dwelling," in *Postmodern Cities and Spaces*, eds., Sophie Watson and Katherine Gibson (Oxford: Blackwell Publishers, 1995), 55.
11. Debra Coleman, "Introduction," in *Architecture and Feminism,* Eds. Debra Coleman, Elizabeth Denza and Carol Henderson (New York: Princeton Architectural Press, 1996), xiv.
12. Nicole Pohl, *Women, Space, Utopia, 1600-1800* (Burlington: Ashgate Publishing Company, 2006), 141.
13. Leslie Peirce, "Beyond Harem Walls: Ottoman Royal Women and the Exercise of Power" in *Gendered Domains: Rethinking Public and Private in Women's History*, ed. Dorothy O. Helly and Susan M. Reverby (New York: Cornell University Press, 1992), 9.
14. Ibid., 20.
15. Maria Pia Pedani, "Safiye's Household and Venetian Diplomacy," *Turcica*, 32 (2000): 11-15.
16. Andrea, *Women and Islam in Early Modern English Literature*, 23. For more see Bernard Lewis, *Istanbul and the Civilization of the Ottoman Empire* (London: University of Oklahoma Press, 1963), 76, 166.
17. Ibid., 24.
18. See Richard Hakluyt, *The Principal Navigations, Voyagers, Traffiques and Discoveries of the English Nation,* 12 vols. (New York: Anis Press, 1965), vol. 6: 114-117.
19. Andrea, *Women and Islam in Early Modern English Literature*, 24.

NOTES

20. See S. A. Skilliter, "Three Letters from the Ottoman 'Sultana' Safiye to Queen Elizabeth I," *Documents from Islamic Chanceries*, Oriental Studies III, first series, ed. S. M. Stern (Oxford: Bruno Cassirer, 1965), 130-31.
21. Andrea, *Women and Islam in Early Modern English Literature*, 24.
22. Skilliter, "Three Letters from the Ottoman 'Sultana' Safiye to Queen Elizabeth I," 131-132.
23. Hakluyt, *The Principal Navigations*, vol. 5: 169.
24. Andrea, *Women and Islam in Early Modern English Literature*, 25.
25. Skilliter, "Three Letters from the Ottoman 'Sultana' Safiye to Queen Elizabeth I," 131.
26. Ibid., 131.
27. Andrea, *Women and Islam in Early Modern English Literature*, 25.
28. Skilliter, "Three Letters from the Ottoman 'Sultana' Safiye to Queen Elizabeth I," 132.
29. Ibid., 132.
30. Leslie P. Peirce, *Women and Sovereignty in the Ottoman Empire* (New York: Oxford University Press, 1993), 415.
31. Ibid., 415.
32. Skilliter, "Three Letters from the Ottoman 'Sultana' Safiye to Queen Elizabeth I," 132-133.
33. Ibid., 132-133.
34. Ibid., 132-133.
35. For more on these alterations to Safiye's letter see Matthew Dimmock, *New Turkes: Dramatizing Islam and the Ottomans in Early Modern England* (Aldershot, UK: Ashgate, 2005), 89.
36. Andrea, *Women and Islam in Early Modern English Literature*, 26.
37. Hakluyt, *The Principal Navigations*, vol. 5: 169.
38. Andrea, *Women and Islam in Early Modern English Literature*, 26.
39. Ibid., 26.
40. Ibid., 26.
41. Skilliter, "Three Letters from the Ottoman 'Sultana' Safiye to Queen Elizabeth I," 121.
42. Ibid., 121.
43. Ibid., 121.
44. Ibid., 123.
45. Luschenko, "The Correspondence of Ottoman Women during the Early Modern Period," 61.
46. Skilliter, "Three Letters from the Ottoman 'Sultana' Safiye to Queen Elizabeth I," 122.
47. Ibid., 148.
48. For more on this see F. Suleman, "Islamic Art at the British Museum: Strategies and Perspectives," in *Islamic Art and the Museum - Approaches to Art and Archaeology of the Muslim World in the Twenty-First Century*, eds. B. Junod, G. Khalil, S. Weber, G. Wolf (London: Saqi Books, 2013), 276-284.
49. Skilliter, "Three Letters from the Ottoman 'Sultana' Safiye to Queen Elizabeth I,"122.
50. Ibid., 133.
51. Ibid., 134.
52. Ibid., 133, 134.
53. Ibid., 139.
54. Ibid., 139.

NOTES

55. Ibid., 139.
56. Ibid., 146.
57. For more on this see Jane Arnold, *Queen Elizabeth's Wardrobe Unlock'd* (London: Routledge, 1988).
58. Pierre Bourdieu, *Language and Symbolic Power*, ed. John B. Thompson, trans. Gino Raymond and Matthew Adamson (Cambridge, MA: Harvard University Press, 1994), 14.
59. Andrea, *Women and Islam in Early Modern English Literature*, 27.
60. Hakluyt, *The Principal Navigations*, vol. 5: 150.
61. Skilliter, "Three Letters from the Ottoman 'Sultana' Safiye to Queen Elizabeth I," 151.
62. Andrea, *Women and Islam in Early Modern English Literature*, 28.
63. Ibid., 28.
64. John Sanderson, *The Travels of John Sanderson in the Levant, 1584-1602*, edited by Sir William Foster (London: Hakluyt Society, 1931), 186.
65. John Mole, *The Sultan's Organ: The diary of Thomas Dallam, 1599 – London to Constantinople and adventures on the way* (London: Fortune Books, 2012), 63.

4. 'SIYER-I NEBI' AND THE EARLY MODERN OTTOMAN REPRESENTATIONS OF MUSLIM WOMEN

1. See 'Siyer-i Nebi: The Life of the Prophet,' *Antika, The Turkish Journal Of Collectable Art*, 15 (1986), accessed April 13, 2014, http://www.ee.bilkent.edu.tr/~history/Ext/prophet.html
2. See *Antika, The Turkish Journal Of Collectible Art*, June 1986; also see Sheila S. Blair and Jonathan M. Bloom, *The Art and Architecture of Islam, 1250-1800* (New Haven and London: Yale University Press), 1996; Carol Garrett Fisher, 'A Reconstruction of the Pictorial Cycle of the "Siyar-i Nabī" of Murād III', *Ars Orientalis*, Vol. 14 (1984): 75-94, Freer Gallery of Art and University of Michigan, accessed April 16, 2014, http://www.jstor.org/discover/10.2307/4629330?
3. See Carol Garrett Fisher, 'A Reconstruction of the Pictorial Cycle of the "Siyar-i Nabī" of Murād III,' *Ars Orientalis*, Vol. 14 (1984): 75.
4. Fisher, 'A Reconstruction of the Pictorial Cycle of the "Siyar-i Nabī" of Murād III,' 75.
5. Qur'an: 33:6.
6. Fisher, 'A Reconstruction of the Pictorial Cycle of the "Siyar-i Nabī" of Murād III', 75.
7. Zeren Tanındı cited in Fisher, 'A Reconstruction of the Pictorial Cycle of the "Siyar-i Nabī" of Murād III', 75, 80-81. It must be stated that the name Muhammad will be used to differentiate the person before his Divine mission as a prophet.
8. Reşit Haylamaz, *Khadija: The First Muslim and the Wife of the Prophet Muhammad*, trans. Hülya Coşar (New Jersey: Tughra Books, 2010), 26-32.
9. His father passed away before he was born.
10. Haylamaz, *Khadija*, 30-31.
11. For more see Godfrey Goodwin, *The Private World of Ottoman Women* (London: Saqi Essentials, 2006).
12. For more see Eric R. Dursteler, *Venetians in Constantinople: Nation, Identity, And Coexistence in the Early Modern Mediterranean* (Baltimore: The John Hopkins University Press, 2006).

NOTES

13. See Leslie P. Peirce, *The Imperial Harem: Women and Sovereignty in the Ottoman Empire* (New York: Oxford University Press, 1993), 28-113.
14. See Qur'an, 33:6.
15. "The prophet is closer to the believers than their own selves, and his wives are their mothers". (Qur'an, Chapter 33, verse 6) This Surah (chapter 33) establishes the dignity and position of the Holy Prophet's wives, who had a special mission and responsibility as Mothers of the Believers. They were not to be like ordinary women: they had to instruct women in spiritual matters, visit and minister to those who were ill or in distress, and do other kindly offices in aid of the Prophet's mission. See Abdullah Yusuf Ali translation of the Qur'an.
16. Mihrimah, her mother Hürrem and her aunt Shah Sultan have been compared to the mystic Sufi woman Rabi'a from Basra (d.801) in their *vakfiyas*. See Esad Efendi, *Osmanlılarda Töre ve Törenler*, edited by Yavuz Ercan (Istanbul: Tercüman, 1979), 3.
17. St. H. Stephan, 'An Endowment Deed of Khaseki Sultan, Dated the 24th May, 1552, *Quarterly of the Department of Antiquities in Palestine* 10 (1944): 170-94.
18. Luce Irigaray, *The Sex Which Is Not*, translated by Catherine Porter and Caroline Burke (Ithaca, New York: Cornell University Press, 1985), 76.
19. Ömer Düzbakar, 'Charitable Women And Their Pious Foundations In The Ottoman Empire: The Hospital of the Senior Mother, Nurbanu Valide Sultan,' (Uludağ University, Faculty of Arts and Sciences, Department of History, Bursa, 2006), 5, accessed March 19, 2014, https://www.ishim.net/ishimj/910/JISHIM%20NO.10%20PDF/03.pdf.
20. Talikizade, *Sehname* (Istanbul: Topkapi Sarayi Muzesi), fol. 29v-30r.
21. Zubayda was one of the great women builders of the Abbasid period. See Kemal Edip Kürkçüoğlu, *Süleymaniye Vakfiyesi* (Ankara: Vakıflar Umum Müdürlüğü, 1962), 46.
22. Doğan Kuban, *Ottoman Architecture* (Suffolk: Antique Collectors Club Distributors, 2010), 263.
23. John Sanderson, *The Travels of John Sanderson in the Levant 1584-1602*, ed. William Foster (London, The Hakluyt Society, First Edition, 1931), 77.
24. Ms. Cicogna 1971, miniature from the 'Memorie Turchesche' depicting the mosque of Haseki Mosque at Avratpazari, (pen & ink on paper), Venetian School, (17th Century) / Museo Correr, Venice, Italy / The Bridgeman Art Library.
25. Kuban, *Ottoman Architecture*, 263.
26. Ömer Lutfi Barkan and Ekrem Hakkı Ayverdi, eds., *Istanbul Vakıfları Tahrir Defteri, 953 (1546) Tarihli* (Istanbul: Istanbul Fetih Cemiyeti, 1970), 341.
27. Nimet Taşkıran, *Hasekinin Kitabi*, (Istanbul: Haseki Hastanesi Kalkındırma Derneği, 1972), 47, 133-34.
28. Necipoğlu, *The Age of Sinan*, 274.
29. See St. H. Stephan, "An Endowment Deed of Haseki Sultan, Dated the 24th May 1552", *Quarterly of the Department of Antiquities of Palestine* 10, 1944, 175.
30. Deniz Mazlum, *Dünden Bügüne Istanbul Ansikplopedisi*, vol. 7 (Istanbul: Tarih Vakfı, 1993), 344-345.
31. Doğan Kuban, *Istanbul Yazıları* (Istanbul: Yapı Endüstrisi Merkezi Yayınları, 1998), 97. Mihrimah was cited as 'Hanim Sultan' (Lady Sultan) whereas her mother Hürrem as 'Haseki Sultan' because she never became the *valide* as she died in 1558 before her son Selim II ascended the throne in 1566.
32. Godfrey Goodwin, *A History of Ottoman Architecture* (London, UK: Thames and Hudson, 1971), 213. Godfrey Goodwin lists the buildings in the Üsküdar Mosque of Mihrimah Sultan, see page 212.

NOTES

33. Ramazanzade Mehmed cited in Necipoğlu, *The Age of Sinan*, 304.
34. Mihrimah, her mother Hürrem and her aunt Shah Sultan have been compared to the mystic Sufi woman Rabi'a from Basra (d.801) in their *vakfiyas*. See Esad Efendi, *Osmanlılarda Töre ve Törenler*, edited by Yavuz Ercan (Istanbul: Tercüman, 1979), 3.
35. Necipoğlu, *The Age of Sinan*, 302.

www.ingramcontent.com/pod-product-compliance
Lightning Source LLC
Chambersburg PA
CBHW070945230426
43666CB00011B/2567